SUNDAY ADELAJA

WHEN TO PRAY, WHEN NOT TO PRAY, AND WHEN TO STOP PRAYING!

Sunday Adelaja
When to pray, when not to pray, and
when to stop praying

©2018 Sunday Adelaja
ISBN 978-1985133426

Cover design by Alexander Bondaruk
Interior design by Olena Kotelnykova

CONTENTS

INTRODUCTION 7

CHAPTER 1: STOP USING PRAYER AS A
COVER-UP...9

Do we really need to pray more? 11
God is waiting for us to do something as well... 12
Use your power 16
Until you use these god-given tools, don't
Expect him to intervene.. 18

CHAPTER 2: LEARN TO BE A MAN OR
WOMAN OF PRAYER, THEN LEARN WHEN
TO STOP PRAYING..23

Most believers stop at praying only..................... 25
What did Nehemiah do next? 26
Let's rebuild 29
Stay awake to see that what you pray for come
to pass.. 31
Think of the outcome!.. 33

CHAPTER 3: PRAYER IS IMPORTANT, BUT
IT'S ONLY HALF OF THE EQUATION 37

The danger of preaching half-truths 39
God is not in any way against the dignity
of labor 42
Who will rebuild the broken walls? 45
atheist and unbelievers have taken
The responsibility... 46

CHAPTER 4: PATRIARCHS OF FAITH 51

Prayer without work is dead!............................... 53

Here comes the heroes of faith............................ 55

The time for change has come............................... 65

CHAPTER 5: YOUR PRAYER MUST PRODUCE SUBSTANCE **69**

Prayer is universal 70

Praying without ceasing shouldn't be taken literally 72

Prayer is not an end in itself................................ 75

Everyone agrees with it, doesn't make it right ... 77

CHAPTER 6: FAITH IS A PUSHER.................**83**

Faith makes your prayer to be effective 84

Nothing is allowed to die while you are there ... 85

Re-educating the church....................................... 88

This will not be possible, not when I'm here 89

It's time for an army to arise! 92

CHAPTER 7: THERE IS A SHORTAGE OF DELIVERERS **95**

Are you not better positioned to make the world a better place? 97

Where are the prayer warriors of our time? 100

Become excellence minded................................. 102

It's time to start using our geniuses................... 104

CHAPTER 8: YOUR FAITH IS PROVEN BY YOUR ACTIONS **109**

Refuse to be defined by your environment........111

Are you a fan or a player?................................... 113

The turning point..116

The courageous queen Esther.............................118

You are here for such a time as this 120

CHAPTER 9: WHEN NOT TO PRAY! 123

Righteous anger 124

Prepare to fight 126

Are you a deceiver or a believer? 127

You are a deliverer! 129

The power hidden in resolving problems 131

CHAPTER 10: PRAYER, FAITH AND HARD WORK ARE INTERTWINED 137

So, it's time to Stop Praying 139

Put Your Creative Abilities to Work 141

Where is the evidence of your faith? 143

What differentiates the high achievers of today from others? 145

CHAPTER 11: AFTER PRAYING WHAT NEXT? 151

Evils of instant gratification 153

Right now, what next? 154

CHAPTER 12: CAN HE COUNT ON YOU? . 165

This is the evidence of my faith 167

Faith is not some senseless dreams or imaginations 170

The evidence of things not seen 172

Go and make it happen 174

CONCLUSION 177

INTRODUCTION

I can feel the curiosity going through your mind already by picking up this book. You are probably wondering what this could be all about. You mean there is a time to pray, when not to pray and a time to stop praying? Yes, my dear friends.

The concept of prayer is one that has been wrongly misunderstood by many in God's kingdom. We've treated prayer as the only thing required to get us whatever we want in life. That's why you see people going from one prayer house to another for things such as financial breakthrough, deliverance and all sorts of prayer requests. Surprisingly, that's all they know about prayers.

This has made a lot of us see God as only a food vendor or a cash dispensing machine that is always there to meet our needs and nothing more. But nothing could be farther from the truth.

Right here in this book, you will fully understand the true concept of prayers. Why do you need to pray? And what's your role in advancing God's kingdom? After praying, what does God expects from you? You will also come to understand that prayer is not an end in itself. In fact, prayer without work is dead. So, you have a role to play as well.

You are God's ambassador on earth. So, He's not expecting you to sit put in prayer houses all day. We should start asking how we can become useful and instrumental to God in transforming our nations. We should find out how we can contribute our knowledge and expertise in God's salvation plan for our countries because until we all stand up and take responsibility, I can guarantee you that nothing is ever going to change for the better.

You have been praying without working and that's why you are where you are today. You are supposed to come out of that prayer room with concrete understanding and insight into what to do. That's the greatest benefit of prayer. That's your advantage. If a believer stops only at praying, he has simply exercised himself in futility.

If we don't have this dichotomy well spelt out in our minds that there is a time to pray and there is also time to get up from that prayer to work it out, then we are going to have a life that is largely ineffective. Even though you pray a lot, you will fail to produce the necessary result just because you don't know when to pray, when to stop praying and when not to pray at all.

It is rather sad that the result we see in the life of Christians and believers all over the world is nothing to write home about. We have so many Christians. So many believers and our churches are packed full of people, but where is the result? Where is the evidence of our faith?

That's why some unbelievers nowadays find it difficult to have faith in God because they can't see the result of the so-called 'believers.' The unbelievers want to see the evidence and substance of your faith.

So, if the problem is not from God, then where is the problem coming from? It is evident therefore, that we are the ones getting something wrong. Meanwhile, at this juncture, I'll leave you to find out the rest for yourself in the book.

Sunday Adelaja
For The Love of God, Church, and Nation

CHAPTER 1
STOP USING PRAYER AS A COVER-UP

A couple of years ago, I was listening to an interview with Christian leaders in Nigeria. And during the interview, they were asked why the country was not well developed even though it has many Christians. Why does Nigeria as a nation of able-bodied, highly intelligent and industrious individuals still have majority of her population living below the poverty line? Why would we have a nation of high achievers in various fields and spheres of life spread across different nations of the world yet, have their own country in such a pathetic state?

In fact, a notable former governor in one of the eastern states in Nigeria once said, he was on a medical trip to the United Kingdom and to his utmost surprise, the best and the only doctors that were available to treat him were two young men from Anambra State and another one from Osun State. These are states in Nigeria. But these talents have been exported and they have become the best in foreign countries.

Then the question comes again, why would we have a nation of high achievers in various fields and spheres of life spread across different nations of the world yet, live as defeated beings, helpless, hopeless, frustrated and wretched?

Can somebody please guess the answer the Christian leaders in Nigeria during that interview gave? The leaders said, *"We need to pray more."* Can you imagine! You mean we should pray more?

What about the 40 days, 70 days and at times 100 days of prayers and fasting declared at the beginning of every year by the leaders of top Pentecostal churches in Nigeria? What about the weekly prayer meetings attended by thousands and hundreds of thousands and at times they even refuse to go to work because of such prayer meetings?

Can you believe that our workers, students, skilled laborers and other talented people make a large percentage of attendance in those meetings? Could it be that God hasn't heard the cry of about 80 million Christians in Nigeria that troop to churches and religious centers at cross over nights during the New Year eve? What about the several millions of our Muslims brothers and sisters who troop to the mosques and worship centers every Fridays?

More interesting is the fact that this is a culture that the country has been practicing for years. For more than two decades now, Nigeria has topped the chart on church attendance around the world. I mean as far back as 1990 when a survey was carried out by the Institute for Social Research of the University of Michigan in the United States up until the last one recorded in 2013. No single nation in the world beat Nigeria in terms of her commitment and faithfulness to attend church meetings and hold religious jamborees.

It seems to me then, that there must be a problem somewhere. It's either God has closed His ears to the cry of His children or we, as His children are not getting something right. But I choose to go with the second option. The millions of Christians in Nigeria must be missing something. What could it be? I'll tell you!

"The value of persistent prayer is not that He will hear us but that we will finally hear Him."
William McGill

DO WE REALLY NEED
TO PRAY MORE?

Nigeria is one of the most prayerful countries on the planet. They pray constantly. But it's clear that countries don't develop by prayer but by prayer paired with actions. It then occurred to me that we as believers are using prayer as a cover up. And we need to stop if this country is ever to move forward and progress.

It reminds me of the time God told Moses, *"Get up! What are you doing on your face? Take action. Go forward."* (See Exodus 14:15.) Praying and interceding are critical, but they are only half of the equation. Why is God silent in your life? Perhaps because He is waiting for you to act! In that chilling silence perhaps you will learn to take action with the power you already have.

I'm convinced that 75 percent of our prayers are a waste of time. Either we are praying for something God has already done, or we are still praying for something He told us to do. We are waiting on God while He is waiting on us! While all that is required of you is to believe in it and act.

I often hear people say they are expecting a miracle and waiting on God for an answer. Waiting on God is good, to a point. Then it's time to stop expecting miracles and start taking action on the revelation we have received thus far.

The kingdom belongs to doers, not hearers. You can hear God speak all you want, but if you don't do anything, the kingdom does not rightly belong to you. The developing world is a great example of this.

In many third world countries, Christians have succeeded in getting people saved and into the church. There, people dance and worship and pray to God, but those same countries lack kingdom principles in the government, businesses, and social structure of the nation.

Can you believe that Democratic Republic of Congo and Ethiopia follows Nigeria in Africa in terms of the number of Christians according to Pews Research Centre in 2010? Yet, some of these countries are full of faithful believers living in poverty. Nothing changes for the better.

The world of the Christians never collides with the world around them. On the other hand, some non-believing countries are wealthy, well organized, and just, but no longer acknowledge the Lord. Dear reader, it's time to roll up our sleeves and get to work.

GOD IS WAITING FOR US
TO DO SOMETHING AS WELL

Tell me, what will you say of a country like ours? Poverty has risen with almost 100 million people living on less than a dollar ($1, approximately £0.63) a day, despite our numerous prayers and church attendance.

The National Bureau of Statistics said 60.9% of Nigerians in 2010 were living in "absolute poverty" – this figure had risen from 54.7% in 2004. This period coincides with the period our dear country holds the top place in church attendance around the world.

Sadly, the bureau also predicted this rising trend was likely to continue. The level of poverty (productivity index) in Nigeria has maintained a constant rise, reaching its all-time high of 72 percent (72%) by August 2016. This is contained in the latest evaluation report on the economic performance of some countries in Africa, Asia, and the Middle East, by a rating agency, Fitch International.

The productivity scale, used in assessing the GDP and other developing indexes of countries, was said to have maintained a constant decline in the past five years in most countries under reference, with Nigeria recording its worst, jumping from 60 percent in 2015 to 72 percent in the second quarter of 2016.

Child Street hawking is a common sight on streets in Nigeria's cities. Children sell products such as boiled groundnut, fruits, and chips that they carry on trays balanced on their heads. In recent months, the practice has been on the rise. The increase is the result of spiraling poverty and the worsening economic situation.

The International Labor Organization estimates that in Nigeria about 14 million children between the ages of five and fourteen are involved in a form of economic activity. Yet we expect everything to work out because we pray or we need to pray more.

Come on! If you expect everything to work itself out and think you can just sit back and rest, I can guarantee you will soon have plenty of difficulties. Do not expect a harvest if you haven't sown anything.

There are times when you must roll up your sleeves to carry out what God told you in the place of prayers and this is one of such times. Not everything is attained easily. The kingdom of God advances by violence. Christians are made strong by the Word of God, but many attain absolutely nothing because they are not willing to work or fight.

God didn't tell Joshua to defeat his enemies with prayer alone. He said, "Be strong and courageous," and then He sent him onto the battlefield *(Josh. 10:25)*. When we keep back the sword from blood, it turns on us and destroys us.

We have to know how to fight and advance the kingdom. When the devil tells you, "No!" you have to be able to tell him, "Yes!" When everyone around you says, "Impossible!" you have to be in a position to say, "It is possible! By faith, it will surely come to pass."

If you are a timid warrior, you will not take the land God has for you. Your position in society will shrink, and the kingdom of God will lose territory because of you. You may be a giant in the prayer closet but a pipsqueak on the battlefield. Stop escaping into prayer! Stop using prayer as a cover up. Be a prayer warrior but not a prayer hermit.

There is a problem in the land and we can't sit still any longer. You and I must arise and go to work until what we see in prayers begin to manifest in the physical. We must enforce the kingdom of God on earth. He won't come down and build our roads for us.

Tell me please, are you expecting God to come and educate our kids in school? Will He come and build the industries, companies and our businesses? Of course not!

So for as long as we stay idle and wait for God to come and do something about our country, nothing will happen. We have prayed and God hears us. So, it's time to start acting on the instructions we receive in prayers. It's time to come down from that mountain top and work out God's plan on earth.

God is waiting for us to do something as well. This explains why all this while that we have buried our heads in prayers, gone to the mountain tops, locked ourselves in churches for days and weeks and all manner of religious activities, nothing has been happening.

We move from one government to the other and yet no notable change is taking place in the entire country. And all you will tell me is "we need to pray more." We prayed and fasted before the elections, during the elections and we continue praying after the election for the elected officers, so what are you still telling me?

If this is the result of all our prayers in the past years then something must change. We definitely cannot continue in our old ways and expect a different result.

"Insanity: doing the same thing over and over again and expecting different results."
Albert Einstein

If only in all our religious endeavors, we caught a glimpse of the mind of God our country will not be where it is today. If only we will also go out with all our zeal and passion expressed towards religious activities and channeled that same kind of zeal and passion to tackle poverty and all the vices in our society, you will be surprised at what a nation we will be having today.

But what do you expect from a people who will wait on God to build their hospitals and schools, feed the poor on their streets, construct roads to connect their cities and towns, fix their electricity issues and even educate their teeming populations? We need to pray more indeed!

USE YOUR POWER

Many church-minded Christians are timid and passive but think they're being humble. They devote themselves to prayer, but they are really just avoiding the battle. People hide in the prayer closet, and use prayer as a cover up thereby, refusing to go to work and bring to reality the plans that God revealed to them in their prayer closet.

As narrated in my book Church Shift, there was a time when our church needed a permanent place to meet, we prayed for a year and God was silent. That silence bothered me terribly. I couldn't understand why we had prayed and God hadn't done anything. I was still expecting God to do everything for us. I wasn't putting my faith into action.

Finally, God had mercy on me and told me that prayer doesn't do anything by itself. "No matter how much you pray, it's not in my hands," God spoke to my heart. *"The solution is in your hands. I have given you the opportunity. The people of the world don't understand prayer. They understand the language of force. Prayer is for Me, and this is not My situation. It is within your scope of influence to change it. You are on the earth; you have the people and the power. Use your power."*

It was time for us to quit praying, and we did. Our actions led to a favorable resolution to our problem and eventually led to a change in the entire nation. But many people still cling to old ways. They are almost idolatrous of prayer.

The only charts we top around the world are the charts of the poorest nations and the highest with church attendance, meanwhile, there is so much power lying within us. But what you will get and what everyone is saying and believing is "we need to pray more." Then we fold our arms and expect a miracle. What an irony!

While we are busy praying on mountain tops and behind closed doors in our churches, our young and promising chaps are still hawking for survival and millions of our children are out of school. Even those in school cannot boast of quality education and our health institutions are out of shape. And you dare tell me all we need right now is to pray more?

My dear friends, prayer without work is dead! We have been praying without working and that's why we are where we are today as a nation. You are supposed to come out of that prayer room with concrete understanding and insight into what to do. That's why we are believers. This is the greatest benefit of prayer. That's our advantage. If a believer stops only at praying, he has simply exercised himself in futility. Prayer without work is dead.

"Get on your knees and pray, then get on your feet and work." Gordon B. Hinckley

UNTIL YOU USE THESE GOD-GIVEN TOOLS, DON'T EXPECT HIM TO INTERVENE

One of the most powerful words in the Great Commission is the word 'go'

"Then Jesus came to them and said, "All authority in heaven and on earth has been given to me. Therefore GO and make disciples of all nations, baptizing them in the name of the Father and of the Son and of the Holy Spirit, and teaching them to obey everything I have commanded you. And surely I am with you always, to the very end of the age."

Matt. 28:18-20 (NIV)

'Go' is also the most neglected word in the church today. Churches try to bring in as many members as possible to sit and listen to our beautiful rhetoric week in and week out. Then whenever they are faced with any difficulty, we ask them to pray more. This is the direct opposite of Christ's instruction to us, which is to get people saved, train them, and release them to change the world they came from.

I know the religious folks are beginning to rage and get heated right now. I also know that you've read the scripture that says 'pray without ceasing' but I'll address that in the course of this book.

I always tell the members that attend our church that my job and my dream is to "chase" them out of their pews to the harvest field of the world where they all belong. One of my most important duties as a pastor is to just get people to "go"!

You are called to battle. There is no need to keep back your sword from blood. There is a time for you to pray and a time to fight. You need to exit the prayer closet and step onto the battlefield. Until you have done everything you can think or imagine, God won't swing into action on your behalf.

He gave you a mind so you can think great thoughts and an imagination so you can imagine what could be. Until you use these God-given tools, don't expect Him to intervene. You must be faithful with what's within your capabilities before you can expect a miracle.

When you have pulled out your sword, gone into battle, and put actions to the revelations you received in prayer, then you can expect God to do more than you could think or imagine. Learn to be a man or woman of prayer. Then learn when to stop praying. The results will be powerful.

> *"When our wagon gets stuck in the mud, God is much more likely to assist the man who gets out to push than the man who merely raises his voice in prayer—no matter how eloquent the oration."*
> *Dieter F. Uchtdorf*

Before you open to the next chapter, I'll like to tell you the reason and the motivation behind this book.

The reason for this book is to correct the wrong definition people give to prayer and to clearly state the role of prayer in the life of a believer.

Unfortunately, even those who pray struggle to know when to pray, when not to pray and when to stop praying. Believe me, there are times when we are not to pray and there are times when we need to stop praying. And of course, there are times when we need to pray. Just as you learnt how to be a man or woman of prayer, you also need to learn when not to pray and when to stop praying and begin to take action.

NUGGETS

1. It's clear that countries don't develop by prayer but by prayer paired with actions.

2. Why is God silent in your life? Perhaps because He is waiting for you to act!

3. The kingdom belongs to doers, not hearers. You can hear God speak all you want, but if you don't do anything, the kingdom does not rightly belong to you.

4. If you expect everything to work itself out and think you can just sit back and rest, I can guarantee you will soon have plenty of difficulties.

5. Do not expect a harvest if you haven't sown anything.

6. If a believer stops only at praying, he has simply exercised himself in futility.

7. He gave you a mind so you can think great thoughts and an imagination so you can imagine what could be. Until you use these God-given tools, don't expect Him to intervene.

CHAPTER 2

LEARN TO BE A MAN OR WOMAN OF PRAYER, THEN LEARN WHEN TO STOP PRAYING

Sometimes people pray without ever taking action and that is what I'm here to address. There is a time to leave the prayer room and carry out the plans God has revealed to you.

For too many years some Christians have concentrated on prayer only. They believe that God will supernaturally accomplish what they are asking for. But the word of God says that faith without works is useless and dead, according to James 2:17. The kingdom does not advance on prayer alone but on prayer-inspired actions.

> *"I used to pray that God would feed the hungry, or do this or that, but now I pray that he will guide me to do whatever I'm supposed to do, what I can do. I used to pray for answers, but now I'm praying for strength. I used to believe that prayer changes things, but now I know that prayer changes us and we change things."*
> *Mother Teresa*

Wow! What a great quotation from Mother Teresa. No wonder she made so much impact during her life time and even many years after she's long gone. But what gets to me is the part that says *"...I used to believe that prayer changes things, but now I know that prayer changes us and we change things."*

My dear friends, until we realize that prayer only changes us to change things in our environment, nothing is ever going to change. Nowadays, it is very sad that we only hear our preachers tell us that anything we ask God for, He will do for us. They even tell us that anything we confess with our mouths, think about or imagine God can do too.

So, you are telling me that all I have to do in life to be successful is to talk or think and ask God for it, then God will immediately swing into action performing what I say and creating my thoughts and desires. Little wonder why we live in a society where all we know how to do is pray and pray more, meanwhile things are getting worse for all and sundry. What a tragedy!

I cannot over emphasize this point. If we do nothing, it doesn't matter how many times we ask God or think about it, nothing will happen in our country. After we have prayed, we must avail ourselves to be used by God to bring the prayers to pass. God needs us to save nations. He wants those prayers to change you and to push you to action so that you can begin to change things according to what He revealed to you in prayers.

Therefore, instead of sitting and saying we only need to pray more, we should start asking how we can begin to feed the hungry around us. We should find out how we can contribute our quota to reduce poverty in our nation. We should begin to find out, "What can I do? What is my role?" and then we ask for the strength to accomplish it. Until we stand up and take responsibility, I am sorry to say, praying more will not take us to our promise land.

MOST BELIEVERS STOP
AT PRAYING ONLY

Let me share with you a little story from the bible times. Once upon a time, Persia, a powerful nation, ruled the world. And King Artaxerxes ruled Persia. That made him the world's mightiest ruler. One of the king's important helpers was a Jewish man named Nehemiah. Nehemiah worked as the cupbearer to the Persian king - Artaxerxes. His job was to taste the king's food to protect the king from possible poisoning.

At around that time, many Jews had returned from the Babylonian captivity. They were rebuilding Jerusalem. But Nehemiah was burdened by the fact that the city walls were still in shambles. Though still living away from Jerusalem, he communicated with those who were living there. He fasted, mourned and prayed for the rebuilding of the walls of his beloved city. He called upon the mercy of God to help them rebuild the walls of Jerusalem as the people returned to the city of God.

Unfortunately, this is where most of us stop. Most believers stop at praying only. A lot of Christians today, only pray without ever taking action. They never leave the prayer room to carry out the plans God has revealed to them.

Of a truth, I know there are a lot of us burdened about the state of the nation just as Nehemiah was burdened about the broken walls in Jerusalem. But how many of us have taken steps to rebuild the broken walls? Are we not locked up in churches and prayer meetings praying for supernatural and divine intervention? Have we left our prayer houses to have meetings on how to empower our youths and stop corruption?

Nehemiah knew quite alright that the walls of Jerusalem were broken and of course, he prayed and fasted about it. But what he did next is what you need to pay attention to. A lot of us are burdened about the state of things in our dear country but the only answer or solution we recommend is to pray more. I wonder where such revelations are coming from.

WHAT DID NEHEMIAH DO NEXT?

Pay close attention here! You will recall that Nehemiah had fasted, mourned and prayed for the rebuilding of the walls of his beloved city but he didn't stop there.

One day, Nehemiah came before the king with a very sad face. Nehemiah's great grief could no longer be hidden, so the king inquired as to what troubled his servant. The king wanted to know what was wrong. Nehemiah responded that his beloved city was destroyed and in ruins. He asked permission to go and help rebuild the city.

"O king, may you live forever," Nehemiah said. "I'm sad because the city where my fathers are buried is in ruins and the gates have been burned." Nehemiah was talking about Jerusalem, which had been destroyed by war many years before.

King Artaxerxes asked, "What is it you would like?" "Let me go to Jerusalem so I can rebuild it," Nehemiah pleaded. King Artaxerxes kindly agreed. He also gave Nehemiah official letters to protect him as he traveled.

The king helped even more. Not only did the king give him permission, the king gave him the resources he would need to accomplish the task. The king granted military troops, horsemen, letters of passage and even building materials for Nehemiah to use. He gave Nehemiah a letter for Asaph, the keeper of the king's forests. Asaph was ordered to provide as much timber as Nehemiah asked for to build the city walls.

When Nehemiah arrived in Jerusalem, he gathered the city officials and said, "We're in trouble here. The city is in ruins and the gates are burned. Let's start rebuilding." He told them that King Artaxerxes approved and, most important of all, God was on their side.

Nehemiah's faith and enthusiasm must have inspired the people. They agreed, saying, "Let's rebuild." Nehemiah told each family which piece of the wall they should fix.

Did you notice that? Did you take note of the fact that Nehemiah was no longer praying for the city to be rebuilt? He has left the place of prayer and has started meeting with men and women who are supposed to be involved in the rebuilding process.

"Our goals can only be reached through a vehicle of a plan, in which we must fervently believe, and upon which we must vigorously act. There is no other route to success."
Pablo Picasso

Nehemiah has received instructions from God, and now is time to call together the leaders, the visionaries, the builders, the engineers and diligent individuals to be involved in the rebuilding process. This is a stage we are yet to get to in our rebuilding process.

If prayers were to be the sole solution and the only answer we need as believers, Nehemiah wouldn't have left Persia. He would have stayed back and continued praying till today and you will agree with me that nothing was ever going to happen or change.

After we've prayed for our power and electricity sector, it's time to begin to call together our engineers and specialist in our churches and come up with ways that sector can perform better nationally. When we've prayed for the leadership in the country, it's time we begin to encourage the young leaders just sitting still in our churches to be actively involved in the leadership positions in the country.

When we've committed the educational sector into God's hands, it's time to stop praying and start gathering the best of the best together to come up with better curriculum and suggest such recommendations to be effected in our schools.

God is not deaf, He hears us and what we need is not to pray more but to begin to take responsibility to rebuild our nation. You and I need to stop praying and start taking prayer-inspired actions.

When we conclude that all that we need is more prayers, what that means is, God is deaf, so He couldn't hear us the first time we prayed. Far from it, He hears us even before we go to Him in prayers. What is lacking is the fact that we don't know when to pray, when not to pray or when to stop praying and begin to take prayer-inspired actions.

In the sphere of influence where God has placed you, He expects you to be responsible. He expects you to swing into action and bring about his plans there rather than kneeling with your hands in between your thighs and believing that praying more will build our roads or improve our health sector.

LET'S REBUILD

It is time we begin to call back our best hands that have fled the country in search of greener pastures. Instead of organizing special prayer sessions for those seeking for visa or work permit outside Nigeria, it is time we begin to encourage our engineers and medical doctors to return and be involved in the rebuilding process. It is high time our experts and technicians come back home to face the responsibility that is facing us as a people.

We need all the human resources we can possibly pull together now because that is the key to the national wealth and prosperity we all crave. We can't have the literacy rate of our country at approximately 50% in this present age and time and expect that things will change by praying more. Come on here, even if God should build our schools or hospitals for us, will He also work there? Is it God that will set up the structures and probably attend to the sick patients or teach our kids?

My dear brothers and sisters, it is high time we wake up from that slumber. We've been dreaming for too long, let's wake up and act. It is time we took up the challenge and responsibility that is before us today. We are the ones to build our own country. Nobody will do that for us and God will definitely not come down and do it as well.

If we go back to the story of Nehemiah you will discover that he did the same thing. Nehemiah set various men and families in charge of different portions of the project. Instead of one large project where Nehemiah tried to control every worker, he broke the building efforts into groups.

Men were put in charge of smaller portions of the wall. Each family built the portion of the wall that was closest to their own dwelling. The project seemed less overwhelming to them this way.

Right now, I want you to begin to think about how you can be instrumental in enhancing and developing our capacity as a nation. It all starts with taking responsibility for a few within your own sphere of influence. You also need to encourage others and make a commitment to seeing that those around you develop their expertise and competence as individuals.

Do something to encourage the youths around you to go to school and settle for nothing but the best. Do something within your capacity to promote personal development in your own area or field. When we all take this as a common responsibility, I assure you that things will not remain the same in our country again. We must take this seriously if we ever hope to build an enviable country for ourselves. This is how we can begin the rebuilding process by taking action.

We've got to wake up and address this negative religious attitude of praying for everything and doing nothing. This negative attitude that is keeping us beggarly, hopeless and helpless must be addressed urgently in our communities, churches, workplace, mosques, schools and all religious centers. It is an urgent call and we all have to do something about it.

STAY AWAKE TO SEE THAT WHAT YOU PRAY FOR COME TO PASS

Along the way, the news of Nehemiah's return became known to the enemies of Israel. Particularly important in the story were Sanbalat the Horonite, Tobiah the Ammonite, and Geshem the Arabian. They vowed to stop Nehemiah and the Jews from rebuilding the city. Sanballat, and his two friends Tobiah and Geshem, were not Jewish and they didn't want the wall rebuilt or the gates fixed.

As the work went on, Sanballat became very angry. He and his friends mocked the Jews. Tobiah said, "When they're finished building that puny wall, one little fox will make it crumble." Nehemiah didn't answer. Instead, he prayed that God would deal with them.

When their mocking insults didn't have any effect, they plotted together to fight against Jerusalem and cause as much trouble as they could. Again, Nehemiah prayed for God's help. He also placed a guard day and night so they wouldn't be taken by surprise.

The project seemed to go well until it was about half complete. The enemy became more and more worried about the progress. They tried to descend on Jerusalem secretly to fight. Nehemiah and the inhabitants of Jerusalem prayed to God for safety. They prepared for battle.

I thought they prayed already, why do they have to prepare for battle again? Didn't he pray that God should

WHEN TO PRAY, WHEN NOT TO PRAY, AND WHEN TO STOP PRAYING

deal with their enemies? I need an answer, please! Is God not supposed to come and fight for them?

Nehemiah and his men knew better. They knew when to pray and when to stop praying and get ready to fight. They prepared for battle even though God was with them because they are sure of their victory.

Wait a minute! Let's take a closer look at what they did. When Sanbalat, Tobiah, and all their allies saw that the Jews were prepared for war, they backed off their attack. Nehemiah and the Israelites worked with a trowel in one hand and sword in the other. Half were prepared for war while half continued the work of strengthening the walls that were necessary for the protection of Jerusalem.

Through the completion of the project the Jews within the walls never even relaxed enough to prepare for bed. They wore their work and fighting clothes constantly except when they had to be laundered.

Did you see that? They were men and women of prayers but they stayed awake to see that what they prayed for must come to pass. They were men and women who are ready to enforce kingdom principles in their sphere of influence.

"Change your life today. Don't gamble on the future, act now, without delay."
Simone de Beauvoir

Oh my God! Where are the Nehemiahs of our day? Where are the men that will enforce God's plan on earth? Where are the women that truly know for a fact that prayer without works is dead and ineffective? Where are the believers that will rebuild God's own country Nigeria?

THINK OF THE OUTCOME!

While we are been fed with the message of praying for everything, even the problems we can solve with common sense, nations around the world who don't even believe in God are offering us aids. Isn't this an irony to be a nation with the highest church attendance, yet no substance to show for our faith? Isn't it laughable that we earnestly pray to God, yet we lack basic amenities for life?

The Jews worked so hard, they were getting weary. Some became afraid that the enemy would come and kill them while they were working. Still, Nehemiah wouldn't stop the project. He put guards around the workers and reminded them that God was on their side and God is more powerful than any enemy!

Finally, the people finished the wall, and only the doors had to be put into the main gates. When Sanballat, Tobiah, and Geshem heard that there wasn't a gap in the walls anymore, they planned to harm Nehemiah. They sent messages for Nehemiah to meet them at a place called Ono. But Nehemiah knew they were trying to trick him out of the city so they could harm him. He wrote back telling them that he would not leave the work to go visit with them.

The wall was finally finished, and Nehemiah set guards to protect it. He also made a rule that the gates should not be opened until well after the sun came up. Through the night, they were to be shut and barred.

"All men dream, but not equally. Those who dream by night in the dusty recesses of their minds, wake in the day to find that it was vanity: but the dreamers of the day are dangerous men, for they may act on their dreams with open eyes, to make them possible."
T. E. Lawrence

Now that the city was safe, many Jewish exiles from different parts of the world returned to Jerusalem. Nehemiah must have been very happy that he had finished the job God gave him to do, in spite of all the obstacles. He stayed on in Jerusalem and helped the people to always obey God.

Dear reader, how many of us can boldly say we've completely carried out the assignment that God gave us in our places of prayer? Have we not neglected God's work and use prayer as a cover up? Do we truly avail ourselves to be used by God and to accomplish God's agenda? Will I be wrong to say that while we lock ourselves up in night vigils and use one-third of the year to fast and wait upon the Lord, other nations around the world are solving their problems and rebuilding their walls?

This is not a time to pray more. It's time to act upon God's instructions. It's a time to start acting and take responsibility. It is not negotiable, there is the role of God in the affairs of men but yet there is the role of man in the affairs of this world as well.

Come to think of it, what if Bill Gates, who made it possible for everyone to own a personal computer or Martin Luther King Jr. the freedom fighter who fought for the African-American minority, decided to keep praying and pray more? What if Nehemiah never left Persia where he was praying for the walls of Jerusalem to be rebuilt? Think of the outcome!

Imagine our world today without the electric bulbs? From the electric bulb in your room to the incandescent lamps in your office or the street lights, just imagine Thomas Edison was only praying for God to come and invent these things? I'm sure if the Wright brothers were to be alive in Nigeria today, they would have been advised to pray more instead of working on the first airplane to fly.

My message to you today is to learn to be a man and woman of prayer and then learn when to stop praying and start acting on God's agenda. Let believers who use to pray that God will feed the hungry, begin to ask for the guidance on what they are supposed to do to reduce poverty around them. Let believers who use to pray and do nothing, begin to allow their prayers change them and then they go out to cause changes to the glory of God. My dear brothers and sisters, it's time to go ahead and do great things.

In the next chapter, you will discover that prayer is important, but it's only half of the equation.

NUGGETS

1. Until you realize that prayer only changes you to change things in your environment, nothing is ever going to change.

2. After we have prayed, we must avail ourselves to be used by God to bring the prayers to pass. God needs us to save nations.

3. Most believers stop at praying only. They never leave the prayer room to carry out the plans God has revealed to them.

4. God is not deaf, He hears us and what we need is not to pray more but to begin to take responsibility to rebuild our nation.

5. We are the ones to build our own country. Nobody will do that for us and God will definitely not come down and do it as well.

6. It is not negotiable, there is the role of God in the affairs of men but yet there is the role of man in the affairs of this world as well.

7. My message to you today is to learn to be a man and woman of prayer and then learn when to stop praying and start acting on God's agenda.

Chapter 3

PRAYER IS IMPORTANT, BUT IT'S ONLY HALF OF THE EQUATION

If you've been following me carefully, by now, you will agree with me that Nigeria's case is not one that needs more and more prayers. What we need now as a country or Africa, as a continent is men and women who will arise from their prayer closets or come down from the mountain tops where they have been praying and stand up to their feet to accomplish God's plans in that country.

What we need right now, are youths who will take responsibility to rebuild their fatherland. What we need are Christians and believers who have come to realize that prayer is only half the equation because God will not come and rebuild our cities for us while we are on earth. Our nations need more 'Nehemiahs'.

Without the Nehemiahs, it doesn't matter how long we pray. It doesn't matter how many people gather in our churches every Sundays or mosque on Fridays to pray for the country. It doesn't matter how many days or months we fast annually. It takes men to cause changes on earth.

But just in case you are still not sure, let me show you something that will interest you more. I'll use this illustration to buttress my point.

I once came across this story some time ago. There was a man driving on a muddy road. Before long his car got stuck in the mud. And instead of him to come down from the car and look for ways to get his car out of the mud, he sat in his car and began to pray to God for divine intervention.

Did you notice that? His car got stuck in the mud, but he decided to stay in the car and pray. Of course, this is a situation that requires a common sense or just calls for emergency help to tow the car.

But this is exactly what we do when the educational sector and the health sector are in shambles and the political terrain is nothing to write home about. Yes, you can pray for the wisdom but after you've prayed for wisdom, it's time to roll up your sleeves and get to work.

"Do not ask the Lord to guide your footsteps, if you are not willing to move your feet."
Anonymous

We are like a people praying to God for help but we are not willing to move an inch. If your car is stuck in the mud and you think prayer alone will push that car out of the mud, you might as well forget about the car and it will sink further. If we can pray to God for help, we should also be willing to take necessary steps that will bring our prayer requests to reality.

You will recall that Nehemiah was burdened by the fact that the city walls were still in shambles. Though still living away from Jerusalem, he communicated with those who were living there. He fasted, mourned and prayed for the rebuilding of the walls of his beloved city.

He called upon the mercy of God to help them rebuild the walls of Jerusalem as the people returned to the city of God.

And what did he do next? He left the place of prayer and travelled to Jerusalem to make sure and see to it that the prayer produced results. He consulted with those who can help in the rebuilding process, from the King in Persia to the elders in Jerusalem.

Nehemiah set various men and families in charge of different portions of the project. Men were put in charge of smaller portions of the wall. Eventually, the broken walls were completed. That is what is possible when you pray and back it up with action.

THE DANGER OF PREACHING HALF-TRUTHS

I also remember hearing the very touching story of one Jane. She was a law student in one of the universities in the western part of Nigeria. Based on her outstanding performance during her days in high school (popularly called the secondary school in Nigeria) she was able to secure her admission on merit to study law in one of the most prestigious schools in Nigeria. Of course, that came with greater responsibility and more expectations from her parents but she wasn't bothered at all. She knew she was up to the task. After all, she's very hard working.

As she was settling down into her new environment and getting used to her dream course of study in school, one of her senior colleagues introduced her to this campus fellowship in school. After her first visit there, she liked it and decided to make that campus fellowship her place of worship.

After a few weeks of attendance, their first semester exams came knocking and she did excellently well. By this time, she was still a member of the campus fellowship.

Before long, the messages being preached in the church began to sink in. Messages such as there is nothing God cannot do for you. Messages such as God will fulfill all your heart desires. And all you have to do is come to church, never miss a meeting, go on evangelism around the campus, get committed and serve as a leader in the campus fellowship.

After a few weeks into the second semester, some of the leaders in the church approached her. They asked her to join a group or two in the church to enable her effectively serve the Lord. Initially, she was reluctant because she didn't think she would have the time to commit to all the numerous meetings every blessed day of the week, due to the volume of materials she needs to cover to stay top of her class.

The leaders persisted in their requests until she decided to let them know what her considerations were. To her utmost surprise, her concerns were interpreted to mean that she was not committed to serving God. They told her that she was putting her studies before God and being in church is what God expects of all of us. So being a genuine lover of God and someone who doesn't want to appear as being rebellious, she reluctantly picked a group.

On weekdays, she went to class from 8 am till 4 pm as a first year student. On getting back from classes, she would normally take a nap and go to the library from 8 pm till 12 in the midnight studying for the next day. And on weekends, she spends most of her day in the library. Including Sundays, immediately after church services, she takes a nap of about 2 hours and heads straight to the library.

Now, she belongs to a particular department in church and her group in the church usually meets on Tuesdays and Fridays 9 pm to 11:30 pm. Of course, the leader and other members are going to come late on most occasions, so the meeting will exceed the normal time. Technically, she's definitely not going to make it to the library on Tuesdays and Fridays, because she's most likely going to be exhausted from such meetings.

Upon joining a group in the campus fellowship, she was now a worker and as a rule, all workers were expected to be present for Mid-week services on Wednesdays and leaders meeting on Saturdays before the choir members will go for their choir rehearsals.

Wanting to please God first and put Him above her studies, Jane endeavored to attend all meetings and most times she was never late for any of those meetings. Tuesdays, Wednesdays, Fridays, Saturdays and Sundays, she was in church. Mind you, Monday evenings was for visiting members that were absent from church on Sunday and all workers are grouped to visit some set of individuals who were absent from church the day before.

Practically, Jane, the best student in high school and she maintained that same high level of excellence in her first semester had little or no time for herself or her studies anymore, but she consoled herself in that she was doing it all in service to God. More so, her leaders in the church have always told her that God will take care of her academics if only she'll serve Him with all her heart.

Now guess what! She only has Thursdays to read her books even during exams. Will I be wrong to say, she has now become more like a full time church staff?

After all, their pastor always reminded them of how he slept on a day to his exams and he saw answers in his dream. In fact, during exams, the pastor will pray for the pen they were going to use to write their exams. All students were expected to bring their pens to church and the pastor will pray for it. This is the height of religion!

What surprises me is that those pens that the pastor prayed on have never produced a Nobel laureate from their university. So, you are telling me that all a student have to do is to concentrate on church meetings and that will cover up for the hard work needed to produce an excellent student? Come on! Who has bewitched us? This is so sad!

GOD IS NOT IN ANY WAY AGAINST THE DIGNITY OF LABOR

This will take me back to a personal story. During my days in the university, I could remember vividly how my professor told me that I will never learn the Russian language. From that day, even though I prayed, I spent extra 6 hours in the school library after 6 – 8 hours in the class every day of the week from Monday to Friday for the next six years.

While others are going home to relax or to the restaurants to cool off, I will carry my bag and it was always very killing. While everyone enjoyed themselves, I will be the only one in the library for another six hours. I normally finish from the library after 9 or 10 pm at night, so I ate there and when I felt like sleeping, I just put my head down and take a nap for about 5 to 10 minutes and continue reading.

I forced myself to sit in the library to study like this for six years. That discipline also, when I became a pastor made it quite easy for me to be able to take a week out every month and lock myself in the room, no wife, no children, no brother, no sister, no contact with external world to pray for up to 14 – 18 hours daily, reading and studying. For 15 years now, non-stop, I've not missed a month.

So if you are thinking I don't believe in prayers, I'm sure you are getting clearer information right now. But prayer is not going to do everything for you. You can imagine a student trying to substitute hard work in your studies with prayers. It will never work.

After that extremely damning verdict by my professor, I was only left with two options; God and the library. First, I spoke to God about it and decided to stand on His promise in Deuteronomy.

"And the LORD shall make thee the head, and not the tail; and thou shalt be above only, and thou shalt not be beneath…"

Deuteronomy 28:13 (KJV)

I made a deal with God that according to His word I would end up being the head in that school, the first and not the last. The other side of that bargain was that I would put my best effort in the library.

"Roll up those sleeves and work until you see the fruit of your labor. It takes passion, resolve, and a productive work ethic, meeting with opportunity, for you to succeed."
Archibald Marwizi

Ladies and gentlemen, after those years of rigorous hard work, I graduated the best student, doing better than all the Russians and students from ninety-nine other countries. I finished first class with a distinction. And it was the best result in the last 25 years of the university.

Just as Nehemiah, he prayed and worked. Today, he could show us the result of his prayers. I am not by any means demeaning prayers but the young generation should not be trapped in mediocrity by the kind of messages we preach. God is not in any way against the dignity of labor.

How can you tell students that prayers alone will make them pass an exam? How can you sit and watch young and brilliant students neglect their studies because you are obsessed with building the largest church membership?

A people who will expect God to write their exams for them and probably open their heads to put the books there while they only pray, fast and attend religious jamborees in the name of religion, how can we expect them to be involved in solving the problems affecting the nation? Isn't it understandable why the leaders will encourage everyone to pray more?

Jane a promising young talent and very brilliant student failed to even make the top 70 percent in her class at graduation. She even struggled to make it into law school. She ended up adding to the half-baked graduates produced in the country. All these because of the deception of religion and the man-made philosophy that says prayer is the only requirement a believer needs to fulfill God's plans on earth.

WHO WILL REBUILD
THE BROKEN WALLS?

Don't get me wrong, when I say prayer is important, but it's only half of the equation. I'm not by anyway saying a Christian or a believer doesn't need to pray. What I'm saying, in essence, is that every one of us needs to be able to clearly define, when to pray, when to stop pray and when not to pray at all.

Before you condemn me to preaching heresy, think of it, with all our prayers, according to UNICEF, 22,000 children die each day due to poverty. And they "die quietly in some of the poorest villages on earth, far removed from the scrutiny and the conscience of the world."

Infectious diseases continue to blight the lives of the poor across the world. An estimated 40 million people are living with HIV/AIDS, with 3 million deaths in 2004. Every year there are 350 – 500 million cases of malaria, with 1 million fatalities: Africa accounts for 90 percent of malarial deaths and African children account for over 80 percent of malaria victims worldwide.

Around 27 – 28 percent of all children in developing countries are estimated to be underweight or stunted. The two regions that account for the bulk of the deficit are South Asia and sub-Saharan Africa. Can you see that Africa is on the list again?

Now, instead of our children to go to school and study to come up with innovative ideas and solutions to many of the infectious diseases, they are only told to pray more. The malarial drugs we use in the continent today, a good percentage was not discovered in laboratories in our higher institutions because the students and professors are busy praying, casting and binding demons; the same demon God told them He has defeated.

Listen, my dear friend, while there might be a thousand and one things God might be willing to do and see happen in Africa, I am sorry to say that He would be incapacitated if there are no men to carry out His instructions. He would not be able to bring all those dreams and aspirations to pass no matter how many times we fast and pray in a day or even shout on top of our voices.

The walls we are crying to God to come down from His throne and rebuild can only be done if you and I will take responsibility and go and carry out God's plan. The future we all dream of and desire is not about to come from heaven. It is within your reach. You've only refused to take charge. You've only decided to stay put in your prayer closet, neglecting your responsibility in the world.

ATHEIST AND UNBELIEVERS HAVE TAKEN THE RESPONSIBILITY

Since we've resorted to keep praying the more, even atheist and some others who don't even believe in God have taken the responsibility upon themselves. Take, for example, the case of Bill Gates who took it upon himself to eradicate polio totally from the face of the earth.

He set about this mission using the vehicle of his foundation; Bill and Melinda Gates foundation. He partnered with the Global Polio Eradication Initiative made up of 4 spearheading organizations like the World Health Organization (WHO), Rotary International, and the United States Centers for Disease Control and Prevention (CDC), United Nations Children's Fund (UNICEF).

Together with several other partners, they have successfully reduced polio's outbreak by 99% and they are on course to eradicate it completely by the year 2018.

Bill Gates, Microsoft's co-founder. His Bill & Melinda Gates Foundation gave $10.2 billion through 2014 to global health initiatives like fighting AIDS, tuberculosis, and Malaria.

Though, popularly known as Akon among his fans, his real name is Aliaume Damala Badara Akon Thiam, born in 1973. The famous Senegalese-American singer, songwriter, producer, and businessman is known for his R & B – style vocals. According to Forbes, he is one of the most powerful celebrities in Africa.

Akon's solar power initiative aims to bring electricity to 600 Million people in Africa, including the believers locked up in church buildings praying to God to come and intervene in our electricity sector. The Akon Lighting Africa initiative has started the Solar Academy, which will help African engineers harness the sun's energy to produce electricity for the target of 600 million people.

Considering that Africa gets an average of 320 sunny days in a given calendar year, you will agree with me that this initiative is a welcomed development.

I have also been opportune to be invited to attend the high profile Clinton Global Initiative meeting in New York City. We met to exchange ideas about solving global problems. Meanwhile, believers are so buried in church activities that the world around them is completely broken and collapsing, and they continue to pray.

On the other hand, the Facebook family, Mark Zuckerberg and Priscilla Chan said they would give 99 percent of their Facebook shares to charitable causes.

The Chan Zuckerberg Initiative, the limited liability company into which Mr. Zuckerberg and Dr. Chan put their Facebook shares, according to New York Times said it would invest at least $3 billion over the next decade toward preventing, curing or managing all diseases by the end of the century.

Sean Parker, who was president of Facebook when the company was still a start-up, also said he would give $250 million to six cancer centers.

> *"The only way that we reach our full human potential is if we're able to unlock the gifts of every person around the world."*
> *Priscilla Chan and Mark Zuckerberg*

In case you don't know, these ones hardly call upon God to come and solve the world problems. Yet, their efforts have resulted in billions of dollars going toward poverty – abatement programs, and their initiatives are addressing problems God wants to be solved: alleviating poverty, improving health, stopping the religious and ethnic conflict, and taking proper care of the earth.

We may disagree with their means to solving these problems, but how many of us have addressed any issue of global impact with all your prayers? How many of our churches have taken a national problem head on?

The problems and issues these people are addressing mean life or death for countless millions dying of some of these deadly diseases. Tell me, has your prayer fed or clothed the widow whose children have not eaten, talk more of finding something to eat herself?

Yet, the people we regard as unbelievers carry God's burden for the poor, the unhealthy, the prisoner, the orphan, and the downtrodden. They are doing exactly what Jesus would do. Feed the poor, care for the sick and provide light for those living in darkness in remote villages.

What a day that will be when believers will take up their responsibility in their environment and stop using prayer as a cover up!

"Do you want to know who you are? Don't ask. Act! Action will delineate and define you."
Thomas Jefferson

God is earnestly looking for men and women who will arise from their prayer closets or come down from the mountain tops where they have been praying and stand up to their feet to accomplish His plans on earth like Nehemiah did.

NUGGETS

1. After you've prayed for wisdom, it's time to roll up your sleeves and get to work.

2. If we can pray to God for help, we should also be willing to take necessary steps that will bring our prayer requests to reality.

3. Prayer is not going to do everything for you.

4. God is not in any way against the dignity of labor.

5. While there might be a thousand and one things God might be willing to do and see happen in Africa, I am sorry to say that He would be incapacitated if there are no men to carry out His instructions.

6. The walls we are crying to God to come down from His throne and rebuild can only be done if you and I will take responsibility and go and carry out God's plan.

CHAPTER 4
PATRIARCHS
OF FAITH

In opening this chapter, I'll like to touch a little on the topic of faith. We cannot be talking of prayer and neglect this important topic. Certain heroes have achieved significant things putting their faith to work. These are faithful servants of God who knew exactly when to pray, when to stop praying and when not to pray at all. And their lives were more productive that this generation of ours that have decided to pray for everything and wait for God refusing to leave our prayer closets.

I would love to point out some of the things they did that made them stand out from this generation of ours. This generation of ours has become one of a prayerful generation, yet nothing to show for all our prayers. Simply because we have refused to clearly define when to pray and when to leave the place of prayer to carry out God's agenda. Tell me, did Jesus come to die so that we live the rest of our lives praying, with nothing to show for it?

We have sat still for decades waiting on God, while God is waiting on us to accomplish His plans and institute His kingdom on earth. We have stayed too long on the mountain, using prayer as a cover up. We have studied and graduated from the University of Religion and Prayers, yet no certificate to prove that our faith in God is producing results.

Tell me, how on earth can we have a nation with the highest church attendance, yet we still go to nations that profess another god for aids? How is this possible? What on earth can make about 80 million believers pray for a country, yet poverty is on the increase, our graduates have gotten used to unemployment after school that they are tired of crying about it, needless to mention, children who should be in school are still lurking around the streets, even along our church premises hawking just to survive? Is this the salvation God promised us? I'm certain it's NOT!

I believe you are beginning to see that no matter how long we wait, "waiting on God" is not going to change our country. If our prayers have not produced any significant result, it's time we begin to look inwards and check ourselves, what are we doing wrong? What ingredient is missing? And let's correct that.

I strongly believe that the missing ingredient is not that God has now become powerless, neither are His arms short that He can't help us. It's just that the men and women who should enforce His kingdom on earth are carried away with religion and using prayer as a cover up.

The men and women who should change the world and make it a better place have refused to come out of their prayer houses. God is talking to us in our places of prayers, yet no one is willing to leave that prayer room and go out to the world and cause a change.

God is earnestly looking for men and women who will arise from their prayer closets or come down from the mountain tops where they have been praying and stand up to their feet to accomplish His plans on earth like Nehemiah did.

Therefore, instead of sitting put in prayer houses, we should start asking how we can become useful to God in transforming our nations. We should find out how we can contribute our knowledge and expertise in God's salvation plan for our countries because until we all stand up and take responsibility, I can guarantee you that nothing is ever going to change for the better. Prayer without work is dead my dear brothers and sisters.

PRAYER WITHOUT WORK IS DEAD!

If you claim to be a prayer warrior or if you claim to be a prayerful person you must also be a person of faith. This is because it is faith that makes your prayer to be effective. You will recall that the bible in Hebrews 11:1 says,

"Now faith is the substance of things hoped for, the evidence of things not seen."

Hebrews 11:1 (KJV)

Faith is the substance... And what is the substance - evidence, something tangible, something you can produce, something visible. Also,

"For as the body without the spirit is dead, so faith without works is dead also."

James 2:26 (KJV)

Therefore, we can boldly conclude from these scriptures that prayer without work is also dead. So, if you are a person of prayer or a person of faith, it must go together with working hard. Why? This is because there is no faith without work.

These are very popular scriptures but do we really understand what it says? I want you to pay close attention to a few words in those scriptures. Pay attention to the word 'substance' and 'evidence.' And it will be clear to you that anyone that claims to be a person of faith has also to be a hard worker so that he can point to the substance of his faith.

Faith produces substance all the time. If I have faith that I am going to have this piece of cloth, the evidence that I have faith is when the piece of cloth appears. The evidence that I have faith is that I've been able to go get that piece of cloth. When I get the piece of cloth, then it has justified my faith. It means I have faith. My faith has produced a result. Faith has produced it.

Somebody who believes in his prayer will also go out and do whatsoever is necessary for him to get the substance of that prayer. Faith must produce substance; it must also have evidence. Prayer, therefore, must also produce substance.

Dear reader, where is the substance that your faith is producing? Do you just go to church or you truly have faith? If you just go to church and you don't have substance, it is a sign that you lack faith. If you truly have faith, you will have substance.

HERE COMES THE HEROES
OF FAITH

Right now, I'll love to point out a few of God's faithful servants who manifested their faith to do things worthy of mention. It is my firm belief that doing this will enable this generation of believers understands that our faith and prayers must always produce results. It is also my earnest desire that their lives will serve as a blueprint to be emulated by this current generation.

MOTHER TERESA

I'll like to start with the story of Mother Teresa, which you read briefly about earlier on in this book. Mother Teresa (1910–1997) was a Roman Catholic nun who devoted her life to serving the poor and destitute around the world. She spent many years in Calcutta, India where she founded the Missionaries of Charity, a religious congregation devoted to helping those in great need. In 1979, Mother Teresa was awarded the Nobel Peace Prize and became a symbol of charitable, selfless work.

On her arrival in India, she began by working as a teacher; however, the widespread poverty of Calcutta made a deep impression on her, and this led to her starting a new order called "The Missionaries of Charity".

The primary objective of this mission was to look after people, who nobody else was prepared to look after. Mother Teresa felt that serving others was a fundamental principle of the teachings of Jesus Christ. She often mentioned the saying of Jesus,

"Whatever you do to the least of my brethren, you do it to me."

In 1979, she was awarded the Nobel Peace Prize "for work undertaken in the struggle to overcome poverty and distress, which also constitutes a threat to peace." She didn't attend the ceremonial banquet but asked that the $192,000 fund be given to the poor.

For many of us, a believer is someone who prays without ceasing. The more prayerful you are, the more faithful you are regarded to be. Hence, we see Christians nowadays boasting of how many days they fast or how many hours they pray in a day.

While it is very true that a believer is supposed to pray, you must also understand that the proof of an effective prayer is the ability to see the result of your prayer request manifested.

Mother Teresa was burdened about poverty, she had faith, she prayed about it, she believed what Jesus said. But more importantly, she went out to do something that will fight poverty. She was not seated in her room praying all day that God will come and feed the hungry or cloth the orphans. No! She has prayed to God about it and God has given her the go ahead. So, the next thing she did was to put her faith to work through the new order called "The Missionaries of Charity."

Whatever field of endeavor or sphere of life you have a burden for and you've prayed about it, then it's time to begin to work to see that your prayers produce results. Any problem you have identified that you are equipped to solve is your mission field. The solution you have been packaged to deliver to the world is what will be the evidence of your faith.

So as a church, it is high time we began to teach the people that they have to go out there to produce substance for their faith. No one should be allowed to just be a church member without having a real plan on what to do and how to go about it, in the area they are passionate about. No one should be allowed in our churches to just come and sit down.

God is more concerned about the orphan down the street than who plays the drum best in the choir. Jesus will rather go and feed the widow and her children than coming to church to lead praise and worship. My heavenly father is more concerned about taking care of the sick rather than coming to a building very early to serve as an usher.

Churches must begin to measure growth and their success by how many they reach through their members who have taken responsibility for various fields in their community. We need to shift our focus from how many members we gather on a Sunday morning and begin to look for ways to expand God's kingdom and chase our people out of the four walls of a church to affect various areas of the economy positively. Then, we can boldly say that our faith is producing results.

GEORGE MUELLER

George Mueller (1805 – 1898) born in Prussia. Prussia was the name for a place in Northern Europe. It was part of Germany for a while, and included land in Poland, too.

Mueller was an evangelist who established orphanages in Bristol, England after a cholera epidemic. For the next 60 years, he cared for more than 10,000 orphaned and abandoned children.

Rising from a life of sin to become one of the world's most revered Christian evangelists, George Muller was a true son of God. With nothing but his faith in Jesus Christ, he set upon himself the task of establishing orphanages for providing care and education for thousands of orphans.

"Caring - about people, about things, about life - is an act of maturity."
Tracy McMillan

His initial work with orphans started when he and his wife started taking in orphaned girls into their rented house. Gradually their work expanded and soon they were managing three homes, not just for orphaned girls, but also for boys and smaller children.

As the population of orphans grew, neighbors began to complain about the noise and Mueller decided to establish separate buildings for the orphanages. He had a very deep faith in God and prayed to the almighty to give him the funds for accomplishing this aim.

He is most respected and remembered for establishing the Orphan Houses at Ashley Down which could accommodate around 2,000 children at any one given time. Children in the orphanage were well cared for and educated. More than 10,000 children were taken care of by him during his lifetime.

Imagine that because of George Mueller and his wife alone; about 10,000 orphans had hope for life. I mean Nigeria alone has approximately 80 million Christians, and a statistics released by UNESCO shows that 29.8 million children living in sub-Saharan Africa were out of school in 2011. This is half of the total amount – 57 million – of worldwide children who were out of school in 2011. This clearly shows that if just half of the Christians in my beloved country will take responsibility for a child, I am not talking about ten thousand children here, just one child; no one will be illiterate in our generation.

I believe you are beginning to see from the same angle I'm talking from. I'm not even talking of Nigeria alone. I mean if just 30 million Christians out of the 80 million who gather for church services every Sunday morning will take responsibility for a child, illiteracy will be a forgotten issue.

How much more can we do if the remaining 50 million Christians set up NGOs to tackle the issue of corruption, fight injustice, encourage family values and another organization is helping the youths to acquire necessary skills and knowledge? Our faith must begin to produce results. We cannot continue to pray more when the society we live in is falling apart.

This goes to show you how relevant the church is in the transformation of nations if we woke up. This also shows you how much we are depriving the world at large by our insensitivity and selfishness demonstrated in the way we do church today.

Have you been praying, then where are the substances that your prayers have produced? Show me the results? Prayer without work is dead. Where is the substance your faith is producing? If you cannot point out the substance your prayers have been producing, then, it's because you did not work it out.

SIR ISAAC NEWTON

Isaac Newton (1642 – 1727) English physicist and mathematician whose many accomplishments include the discovery of the law of gravity and the invention of calculus.

Sir Isaac Newton was born in the city of Lincolnshire, England in 1643. His father died just months before he was born, and when he was three years old, his mother left him in the care of his grandmother. Isaac was always a top student and went off to the University of Cambridge at age 19.

While at Cambridge, Newton was influenced by the writings of Galileo, Nicholas Copernicus, and Johannes Kepler. By 1665, Newton began developing a mathematical theory that would lead to the development of calculus, one of the fundamental branches of mathematics. Newton would also go on to discover other important math theories such as Newton's Identities and Newton's Method.

In 1670, Newton moved on to the study of optics and developed theories relating to the composition of white light and the spectrum of colors. In one of his famous experiments, he refracted white light with a prism, resolving it into its constituent colors: red, orange, yellow, green, blue, and violet.

As a result of his experiments, he developed Newton's Theory of Color, which claimed that objects appear certain colors because they absorb and reflect different amounts of light. Newton was the first scientist to maintain that color was determined solely by light, and his findings created much controversy. Most scientists thought that prisms colored light.

Nevertheless, Newton then created the world's first color wheel, which arranged different colors around the circumference of a circle. He is also credited as the first scientist to explain the formation of a rainbow – from water droplets dispersed in the atmosphere.

In 1679, Newton continued his work on gravitation and its effects on the planets. In 1687, he published Philosophiae Naturalis Principia Mathematica. In this landmark work, Newton explained his three laws of motion, which included his theory of gravity.

According to Newton, gravity is the reason that objects fall to the ground when dropped. Moreover, gravity is the reason why planets orbit the sun, while moons orbit planets, and why ocean tides exist. Newton's theories remain among the most important concepts in the history of science.

There is some evidence that Newton's ideas concerning gravity were inspired by apples falling from trees. There is no evidence to suggest, however, that any of the apples hit him on the head (as cartoons and fables suggest).

Below are Newton's three laws of motion:

1. Newton's First Law (Law of Inertia) states that an object at rest tends to stay at rest and that an object in uniform motion tends to stay in uniform motion unless acted upon by an external force.

2. Newton's Second Law states that an applied force on an object equals the time rate of change of its momentum.

3. Newton's third Law states that for every action there is an equal and opposite reaction.

Following the publication of his work, Newton became instantly famous throughout Europe. In the later years of his life, he wrote several articles on the interpretation of the bible. He was also appointed a member of the British Parliament and spent many years reforming the Royal Mint (coin making agency of Parliament). He died on March 20, 1727.

> *"Atheism is so senseless. When I look at the solar system, I see the earth at the right distance from the sun to receive the proper amounts of heat and light. This did not happen by chance."*
> *Isaac Newton*

Newton's understanding of God came primarily from the Bible, which he studied for days and weeks at a time. The motion of an aircraft through the air can be explained and described by physical principles discovered over 300 years ago by a man who had faith and believed in the same God we preach today. He was only 23 years old when he developed the theories of gravitation.

Wait a minute; don't you think there might just be someone behind closed doors praying all day who can help in developing principles that will be the blueprint for future technological discoveries? Tell me, as believers are we not meant to have access to eternal wisdom more than the unbelievers who are ruling and leading the world of science and technology today?

But what else can we expect? Even though God reveals such to you, will you leave your prayer closet to go and perform that experiment in the laboratory? Won't it be regarded as being carnal by your church leaders? Has church attendance not become more important than studying and making scientific discoveries?

If Isaac Newton could transform the world through his discoveries and he still studied the bible and prayed, then when did it become a taboo to spend hours in the library or laboratory? Why have we glorified attending church meetings over what can make the world a better place?

As a believer living in this age, what legacy are you going to leave behind? Will you be able to point to one concrete thing your faith produced? Or you will look back and the only thing you can point to is the number of church meetings you attended or the number of days you fasted and prayed, waiting for God to do what He has commissioned you to do?

MARY SLESSOR, HEROINE OF CALABAR

Talking about legacy, Mary Slessor is most likely the reason why you are alive today, especially if you were born a twin from Nigeria. Mary was born in the city of Aberdeen, Scotland. She loved to read and there were many delightful books in the Sunday school library. The stories of Livingstone in Africa were especially interesting to her.

Mary's heart was stirred by a missionary from Africa who came to their little church and told of his experiences. As she listened, her eyes growing large and round, she said to herself, *"I wish I could do something to help those children. I am going to be a missionary when I grow up, and go out there and teach those folks the right way."* She dreamed of Africa.

Finally, in 1875, she applied to the Foreign Mission Board of her denomination for a place in Calabar, Cross River state, Nigeria. The position was granted for there was a need for workers at that station. Mary had a dauntless spirit. She felt that with God's help she was a match for any problem that might stand in her way.

She was now twenty-eight years old. God led her into the jungles where she brought many savages under the Gospel's power single-handedly. As a preparatory step for the time when she was to carve a career for herself that was unmatched by any woman missionary, she worked in the coast town of Calabar. Before she died God took her where no white man even had trod.

The twin murder superstition of the Dark Continent, which caused parents to murder one of the twins born to them, thinking that it was devil-sent, was an evil which Mary hated. One day a twin which had been left for dead was brought to her. Mary took the child into her home as her own. This was the beginning of a marvelous career of twin-rescuing which finally resulted in the natives abandoning the practice entirely.

Dear reader, look around you and tell me, what is the church of today doing about the challenges of the people around them? What are the believers, faith-filled and tongue talking Christians doing today to tackle the evil practices in their field? How many of us prayer warriors are actually doing something tangible to affect our environment like we saw the likes of Sir Isaac Newton, Nehemiah, Mary Slessor, Mother Teresa did? Instead, we are busy praying and encouraging others to pray more when the lives we should be focused on building aren't getting better. What a tragedy!

Sometimes, I wonder! Are we really praying to the same God the believers of old also prayed to? If so, why don't we have tangible results and concrete evidence to back up over faith?

THE TIME FOR CHANGE
HAS COME

The time for change has come. The time to take the believers to a whole new level and realm of operation is here now. I challenge you; I challenge the ministers of God, pastors, bishops, and all spiritual leaders in their entirety to discover the mind of God in prayer and see to it that we build according to the pattern that God has shown us.

If you claim to be a prayer warrior or if you claim to be a prayerful person you must be a person of faith. Somebody who believes in his prayer will also go out and do whatsoever is necessary for him to get the substance of that prayer. Faith must produce substance; it must also have evidence. Prayer, therefore, must also produce substance.

God is earnestly looking for men and women who will arise from their prayer closets and stand up to their feet to accomplish His plans on earth like the patriarchs of faith.

The time has come when the men and women who should change the world and make it a better place start to come out of their prayer houses. God is talking to us in our places of prayers, and we must be willing to leave that prayer room and go out to the world and cause a change.

"Do and act on what you believe to be right, and you'll wake up the next morning feeling good about yourself."
Janet Reno

I will be elaborating more on the practical steps you can take to begin making a difference big time in the next chapter. Your faith is dead if it's not producing any substance. Therefore, you must know when to pray and when to stop praying to go and work out your faith.

NUGGETS

1. This generation of ours has become one of a prayerful generation, yet nothing to show for all our prayers.

2. If your prayers have not produced any significant result, it's time you begin to look inwards and check yourself, what am I doing wrong?

3. God is talking to us in our places of prayers, yet no one is willing to leave that prayer room and go out to the world and cause a change.

4. Faith makes your prayer to be effective.

5. Faith is the substance... And what is the substance - evidence, something tangible, something you can produce, something visible.

6. If you are a person of prayer or a person of faith, it must go together with working hard. Why? This is because there is no faith without work.

7. Faith produces substance all the time.

CHAPTER 5
YOUR PRAYER MUST PRODUCE SUBSTANCE

Having looked at what the patriarchs of faith have accomplished, I am certain you can begin to see the places where you have missed it today and what you can begin to do so that your prayers and faith will start producing tangible evidence.

God is desperately in need. But His needs are not material or some petty mundane things. He is not in need of the same kind of things we need. Rather He is seriously in need of sons, deliverers, mighty men and saviors in the health sector, science, and technology, education, transportation, entertainment, sports and industry who will take responsibility for the affairs of their nation.

God is desperately in need of individuals that will arise to face the challenge of the day and bring about the much needed change in our society beginning with their own area of influence and concern. He is tired of Christians praying and believing that when they pray more something will change.

Most especially, He is tired of seeing non-Christians taking advantage of their human potentials to do great things, while the people who are called by His name are locked up in some buildings on every street crying and shouting in prayers.

Right now, I'll like to take some time to shed some more light on what prayer truly means. I want to also address a few misconceptions that are being perpetuated in Christendom nowadays.

PRAYER IS UNIVERSAL

"To be a Christian without prayer is no more possible than to be alive without breathing."
Martin Luther

The word prayer is so universal that you could hardly see anyone who doesn't know what prayer means. Even in nations where people are supposed to be atheist and agnostics yet the concept of prayer is impossible to hide. This by itself is a proof of the fact that there is a supernatural force which is God in heaven.

As we know, there are quite a number of religions in the world. Many religions abound, just as there are many different people and cultures. To bring it closer home, Africa has its own religion. Our forefathers used to worship some sort of god of nature, the god of the universe, and the God of creation. Our forefathers prayed to their gods before Christianity and Islam were even brought to Africa.

If in every tribe, a group of people and nation on earth, people know the concept of prayer and they will instinctively call out in prayer when in danger that is a fact that we have a God in heaven. Even if it is for selfish reasons, or out of instinct, it is still a proof that there is a God in heaven that everybody instinctively knows is up there that could help and deliver at all times. Therefore, prayer is an affirmation that there is a loving God that could come to the aid of man whenever we are in trouble.

Therefore, in every nation, culture or tradition, prayer is conspicuously present. The problem now is the fact that people now view prayer to the Almighty God as an emergency action but that is not the real meaning or essence of prayer.

Prayer is actually an on-going, loving relationship and communication with a higher power, which is our heavenly father. So, prayer is not just about asking God to help you out in times of need.

The true understanding of prayer is when you look for God because you want to know him and you establish an on-going relationship with Him - a relationship of trust, love and that of a father to a child. That process of communication that goes on in that relationship is what is called prayer.

Prayer could come in form of a worship or meditation. It could also come in form of a request or a petition. The communication involved in prayer could be when you are reading His word also.

For a lay man, prayer is a form of appeal, demand, supplication or even begging for some form of help from God. And you will agree with me that if you are looking to God for help during emergencies alone, then you will pray to any god at all that will help you. When you are really sick and in serious pain, you will allow anyone to be your doctor.

When somebody is in danger, the instinct works in such a way that you don't look for the right God at that time. You are not thinking about loving God at that time, you are not thinking about building any relationship at that time because you are only focused on how you can get out of that situation. So, it is actually egocentrism and selfishness that is driving you.

In short, most people see prayer as necessary only when they need some help. Even though God in His infinite mercies does answer most prayers like this, it is very important that you note the fact that prayer is much more than that.

Sadly, people have been carried away with this superficial idea of prayer that they've lost relationship with God. What they fail to understand is that it is possible to pray every day and go to church regularly and still not have a relationship with God.

PRAYING WITHOUT CEASING SHOULDN'T BE TAKEN LITERALLY

"Pray without ceasing."

1 Thess. 5:17 (KJV)

A careful observation of what Apostle Paul wrote here clearly indicates that this particular bible verse cannot be interpreted literally. If we are to take this scripture literally, we could as well say, we as believers are not going to sleep or work again all because we are so occupied with praying without ceasing.

If we are to take such a phrase as 'praying without ceasing' literally, it probably means we have to be in prayer 24 hours, that could also mean being in the church 24 hours or on your knees in your house 24 hours or at least most of the time.

The question then arises, when do we work? When do we teach others the word of God? When do we sleep?

When do we build houses to live in? When do we have children and when do we raise up these children? When do we study? When do we teach others? When do we do all the things we need to do to make a living? When do we go to work? Remember, the bible also says, if you don't work, you shouldn't eat.

So, what Apostle Paul meant by 'pray without ceasing' means to maintain a continuous relationship with God. I believe you are beginning to see that praying without ceasing cannot be taken literally.

Praying without ceasing, therefore, could only be understood as having a continuous communication with God. That is maintaining an on-going and persistent relationship with God.

Let's now take a look at the way Apostle Paul himself lived his life. It is obvious that he did not just lock himself up in a room or a monastery just praying. His short biography tells us that he was a very busy man and he was still a praying man.

He still had a secular job. Paul was a tent maker. This obviously shows that he had his times of prayer. He was also a prolific teacher and writer. Certainly, when he was teaching, he was not praying without ceasing at that time. The same thing could be said when he was writing his numerous letters to the churches.

It is completely inconceivable to think of him praying while talking and fellowshipping with people. Without any doubt, the term 'praying without ceasing' was not a fanatical phrase in the understanding of Apostle Paul like some Christians want it to be today.

Unfortunately, this is a far cry from what we often see in some highly religious Christian movements to-

WHEN TO PRAY, WHEN NOT TO PRAY, AND WHEN TO STOP PRAYING

day. The patriarchs of faith knew when to pray and they also knew when to go to work. They knew when to go to the church and do their Christian duties and they knew when to leave the church and go out there to deliver what they've prayed about. They knew when to go to the mountain and receive power, but they also knew when to leave that same mountain and go to the secular world to establish the kingdom of God.

What you get in the place of prayer must be used to advance the kingdom of God. Your prayer must produce substance. Prayer is not an end in itself. You get God's insight, power, resources, energy, and understanding in prayer so that you can take it to the secular world and establish His kingdom there.

When you refuse to work, are you now going to pray to God to help you with your rent and bills? Have you not turned God to an ATM machine or your food vendor? It is when you work that you deserve to eat. Faith without work is dead, just as prayer without work is equally dead.

When you continually fellowship with God, you can never lack answers on pressing problems in your society. When you perpetually communicate with God through worship, study or reading His word, you can never end up a mediocre. When you have an on-going relation-ship with God, you can never be forgotten. This is what prayer is all about.

Praying without ceasing, therefore, could only be un-derstood as having a continuous communication with God. That is maintaining an on-going and persistent relationship with God. If you have a continuous com-munication with God and maintain an on-going and persistent relationship with Him, your life can never be without proves of your faith. It will always produce results.

That is why people who only go to God in times of need barely have anything to show for their years in the church. Instead of maintaining an on-going relationship with God, they go to Him always because they have a pressing need. If you think this is not true, listen to yourself the next time you pray. Your prayer is filled with what will benefit you and those around you alone.

But show me a man who have closely walked with God and maintained a continuous relationship with Him, and I will show you a patriarch of faith.

PRAYER IS NOT AN END IN ITSELF

If all you've known about prayers is what you can get from God through it, then you've been eaten up by selfishness and paganism. Most idol worshippers only go to their god whenever there is danger and they are in serious trouble. Now tell me, if you only go to God to meet your needs are you any different?

God has needs also. He wants to feed the orphan on your street. He wants those children out of school to have access to education. He wants that widow next door to understand what it means to be comforted. He wants the institution of marriage to be respected and stabilized around the world. He still loves sinners and He is in need of laborers to go out there and show them love. And most importantly, He needs you and me to carry out these assignments.

So, the next time you go to Him in prayers, just as you want Him to meet your needs, He also wants you to listen to Him and carry out His instructions in your sphere of contact. Don't just seat in the place of prayers screaming for what you want Him to do for you.

Jesus once said in John 5:17, *My Father has been working until now and I too am working.* But this is the same man that always leaves His disciples to pray. This is because He knew that there is a time to pray and a time to stop praying. He knew that there is a time to receive instructions in the place of prayer and a time to carry out such instructions on earth. He was on the mountain at night praying, but He always came down to do the work of His father that sent Him.

"There is no substitute under the heavens for productive labor. It is the process by which dreams become realities. It is the process by which idle visions become dynamic achievements."
Gordon B. Hinckley

When a man knows the time to stop praying and leave that prayer corner to carry out God's plans, he can never know mediocrity or lack evidence of his faith. Little wonder, Jesus' life was full of evidence. His faith produced results and it is still visible to the blind two thousand years later.

Isn't it evident that the believers today are so ineffective in causing a revolution in our world? How can a people who are so busy praying ever get to make a difference in a society? How can a people who are so detached from their environment ever get to make the world a better place? There is just isn't anyway to make that happen.

Whereas children of God ought to be trained, equipped, developed and raised to be saviors and messengers of hope to the hopeless. Christians who are responsible for themselves and their society at large, they have become so removed from the same society they've been called to deliver from the bondage of poverty and lack.

For too many years we have concentrated on prayer alone. We have wrongly believed that God will supernaturally accomplish all that we ask of Him. But the word of God says that faith without works is useless and dead.

My dear friend, prayer is not an end in itself. The kingdom does not advance on prayer alone but on prayer-inspired actions. Therefore, let's begin to take action on whatsoever we pray about, and then, our prayers will begin to produce substance.

EVERYONE AGREES WITH IT, DOESN'T MAKE IT RIGHT

Another doctrine I'll like to touch on in this chapter is the one that says, "one day of favor is better than ten years of labor." This is a very popular doctrine but also very wrong. The fact that everyone is saying it doesn't make it right.

Even Jesus was always busy and working and God created the heaven and earth in six days, why did He not do that in one day if one day of favor is better than ten years of labor? Jesus' ministry lasted three years. Once again, he didn't operate with this man-made doctrine that says one day of favor is better than ten years of labor.

This is a doctrine that breeds laziness and makes people wait on God because they believe that once that prayer is answered, it's better than ten years of work. Unfortunately, what you learn from ten years of work, you can never learn it in a second of a miracle.

Show me a man that started a business by miracle and I'll show you a man that cannot teach or reproduce that business elsewhere, which makes him dependent on miracles.

But show me a man that built his business in the space of ten years and I'll show you a man that has learnt through those years from his mistakes and have developed a model that is teachable and can be reproduced anywhere else.

"A garden requires patient labor and attention. Plants do not grow merely to satisfy ambitions or to fulfill good intentions. They thrive because someone expended effort on them."
Liberty Hyde Bailey

We cannot continue to promote laziness and false doctrines and expect Christians to be effective and productive. This is the same kind of doctrine that will make students believe that once their prayers are answered, then, they don't need to read again. Or all I have to do to get a financial breakthrough is to keep praying, then, I don't have to do anything else but pray till I get the breakthrough, because one day of favor in prayers is equal or better than ten years of hard work. It is such a shame.

The believer should be trained to become a kingdom carrier and a kingdom imposer in the sphere of life that he is concerned with. He's got to be trained to be an expert in that field. He has to become an authority so that people can listen to him. He needs to acquire all the necessary knowledge to become the very best in that field. The kind of knowledge that will make you a professional, a specialist by every definition, and a master in that field, this is what you should be concerned about.

And where is the best place to encourage people to become the very best in their fields, callings and in their gifts? The church of course! But rather, what do we have in our churches?

Young converts are taught to believe that one day of favor is better than ten years of labor. While we cannot deny the favor of God, we should also note that God is not against the dignity of labor. He is a hardworking God and you shouldn't be any different.

Another bible story that has been used to support this man-made doctrine is the one talking about how the children of Israel left Egypt with so much gold and silver.

Think about it yourself. These same people have been slaves and afflicted for not less than 400 years, so, taking these things was very just because the Israelites had been working as slaves for these people. They had earned the valuables. This was one of God's ways of providing for His people.

We must do away with all these man-made doctrines and philosophies that have no biblical backing. I'm deeply concerned about the children of God who ought to know better and who ought to be taking up the responsibility of fixing the earth but are not doing so. And this is a shame to the body of Christ in general because at least believers go to church; they pray to God, they read the bible. Yet, they have left the affairs of the world in the hands of mostly unbelievers.

The fact is that we are better positioned to change this world but ironically we are the ones who have done worse in exploring the earth than the sons of men who are not even believers. I blame this on the kind of messages and doctrines we are constantly being fed with in our churches.

> *"It is only through labor and painful effort, by grim energy and resolute courage that we move on to better things."*
> *Theodore Roosevelt*

Therefore, messages that emphasize the dignity of labor must return to our pulpits. Messages that are empowering and inspiring contrary to the ones that keep people beggarly and poor should be preached. Messages that challenge God's people to come up with solutions to pressing problems around them should be encouraged.

And this is not for the churches or religious organizations alone because if we are to develop and improve as a nation we must all work together to be stake holders. Therefore, these same principles must begin to replace man-made philosophies in every area we find ourselves. Use any medium at your disposal, your NGOs, and even your social media platforms.

In the coming chapters, I will be showing you how to practically make sure you produce tangible evidence that will vindicate your prayers, using real life models that you can relate with. I will also show you how to start from where you are right now and make a difference in your world like the patriarchs of faith.

We need to begin to produce concrete evidence and substance that will proof our faith and vindicate our prayers. It's high time we began producing the replica of God's kingdom on earth.

NUGGETS

1. God is desperately in need. But His needs are not material or some petty mundane things. Rather He is seriously in need of sons, deliverers, mighty men and saviors in the health sector, science, and technology, education, transportation, entertainment, sports and industry who will take responsibility for the affairs of their nation.

2. God is tired of seeing non-Christians taking advantage of their human potentials to do great things, while the people who are called by His name are locked up in some buildings on every street crying and shouting in prayers.

3. Prayer is an affirmation that there is a loving God that could come to the aid of man whenever we are in trouble.

4. Prayer is actually an on-going, loving relationship and communication with a higher power, which is our heavenly father.

5. The true understanding of prayer is when you look for God because you want to know him and you establish an on-going relationship with Him - a relationship of trust, love and that of a father to a child.

6. Praying without ceasing, therefore, could only be understood as having a continuous communication with God.

CHAPTER 6
FAITH IS A PUSHER

Having understood the true meaning of prayer, it's time to build on it. Let's take it a bit further as I shed more light on the topic of faith.

Faith is a pusher to go and work. Faith is what does not permit you to sit down and wait for only God knows when. Faith is what energizes you to keep on working, laboring, and searching till you find the missing piece. A person filled with faith is always a workaholic. That's the same also with a man of prayer.

> *"Faith is not a superstition or an intention; it is action."*
> *Benson Idahosa*

What am I saying in essence? If I have faith, I'll go look for what it is I'm praying for. If I really believe I can find it, that faith and assurance in me become a propeller for me. That assurance becomes a motor or an engine that is propelling me.

If I have faith that I am going to get something, I must stand up from where I am and work to produce it. The work here may mean to go look for it. Work could also mean to build a factory to produce it.

I must work to get it. If I am praying for something to come, my prayer gives me the faith that I will find it.

And I will go and do everything necessary to get it. That is faith in action.

FAITH MAKES YOUR PRAYER
TO BE EFFECTIVE

For reference sake, read Hebrews 11:1 once again.

"Now faith is the substance of things hoped for, the evidence of things not seen."

Hebrews 11:1 (KJV)

From this scripture, it is evident that a man of faith is also a man of substance. I want that to sink in. If you don't get it, you might want to read it again. A man of faith is a man of substance, which also means a man of prayer must be a man of substance as well. This is because it is faith that makes your prayer to be effective.

The bible called Abraham to be a man of substance. Isaac was a man of substance. Jacob was also a man of substance. David was a man of substance too. A careful observation of their lives will prove that as well. These people have something to call substance. They have something to show for their walk with God. They have something that proves their faith.

If anyone calls you a man of substance, it means that you have something to show for it. To be a man of substance also means to have something to display. Are you truly a man of faith? Do you have any substance to show for it?

Oh, how I wish that you will see from this point of view as well. I am talking about real faith here, not any other type of faith that can't produce any result.

For example, people from Nigeria refer to Archbishop Benson Idahosa as a man of faith. We see the substance the man produced with his life. A man of faith is a man of substance. What are the substances that your prayer is producing? Where is the substance that your faith is producing?

How I wish that you will begin to see that God has already equipped you with the solution and answers to all the troubles around you. This is why I am writing to you right now. This is what I want you to see.

I want you to understand that as a nation, we are well able to handle the challenges of the day. We have the capacity to deal decisively with every single problem facing us. We have all it takes to keep things under perfect control in our land. And it is time we began to do something in this regard.

"Action is the foundational key to all success."
Pablo Picasso

NOTHING IS ALLOWED TO DIE
WHILE YOU ARE THERE

One man's story I'll like to share with you in this chapter is that of Archbishop Benson Idahosa. He was a man of uncommon faith, and a model to the lukewarm believers of today, who believe that prayers alone will accomplish all that they desire and want to see happen on earth.

Nigeria is the home of several notable men of God, but I do believe that none has made such an international impact as the late Benson Idahosa affectionately called PAPA by his followers.

Idahosa was a Charismatic Pentecostal preacher, and founder of the Church of God Mission International with headquarters in Benin City, Nigeria. He was the first Pentecostal Archbishop in Nigeria and is often referred to as the father of Pentecostalism and televangelism in Nigeria.

Benson Andrew Idahosa was born in Benin, Edo State on September 11, 1938, of poor non-Christian parents in a predominantly non-Christian community.

As narrated by him,

"As a young Christian, I once heard my pastor say during a morning service that Christians could raise the dead in the name of the Lord Jesus Christ.

And flying around on my bicycle in those days, I went through the city of Benin in search of a dead person to raise to life.

After about five hours of hard searching, I found a compound where a little girl had died a few hours before. The corpse had been cleaned and prepared for burial. I walked boldly up to the father of the dead child. "The God whom I serve can bring your baby back to life," I told him. "Will you permit me to pray for the child and bring her back to life?"

The man was startled, but he agreed. With great enthusiasm, I walked into the room and up to the bed. The child was cold and dead. With strong faith in the Lord, I called on the Lord to restore the child back to life. I turned to the corpse and called it by name, "Arise in the name of the Lord Jesus Christ." Oh Glory to God! The corpse sneezed, heavily, alas. The child had come back to life!"

Raising the dead was to become one of the hallmarks of his ministry. In all, it was recorded that he raised 28 persons from the dead at different locations including his meetings and crusades.

Come on somebody! What boldness and audacity this man is demonstrating here! This is exactly what we need in Nigeria, my friends. You mean all he heard was his pastor preach that Christians have the power to raise the dead and that message alone activated the faith in him and pushed him to leave the church to produce results?

Someone should be looking at the mountain of corruption killing our economy and saying I have the solution to this menace because I'm a child of God. Someone else should be looking at the mountain of poor medical care in our country and saying give me this problem I can handle it. You should be looking at our poor transportation and educational system and let your faith push you to make a difference there.

As Christians, no sector of the economy is allowed to die while we are there. As believers, no child should be allowed to roam the streets without a house to sleep or food to eat. Let your faith push you to raise back to life every dead thing that is contrary to God's principles and plan.

We bring life to everything we come across and everywhere we go. You see the educational sector is dying; it's not a time to pray more. Do your research, study and come up with ideas that will revive that sector. You see the entertainment industry collapsing or the health sector cannot sustain itself, then go and find out what the best practices are around the world and come up with ways in which you can apply it to your situation.

If you are truly a man of faith, it will push you to produce result always. The era of having a church packed full
of lukewarm, passive and effortless Christians is over.
Let your faith push you to produce results. Faith is the
substance of things hoped for, where is your substance?
Where is the tangible result you've produced? Where is
the evidence that you have faith? What changes has your
prayer produced?

RE-EDUCATING THE CHURCH

Dear pastors, it's time to start pushing people out of
the pews into their various fields and strata of the society. A lot of these sectors are dying and crying for help.
It's not enough to send people out to the streets to evangelize and bring in more members.

Dear leader in the church, we must begin to send people out to dominate every sphere of influence out there.
Every church has got to draw out a plan and strategy to
completely take over its mandate in establishing God's
principles in our environment.

We need to have plans on how we are going to allevi-
ate poverty and reduce suffering in our society. We need
a clear cut outline on how to raise the next generation of
leaders to be effective and accountable. And this can be
achieved if we have excellent leadership training schemes
as part of our ministry.

I'm not talking about leaders that you are raising to
start another branch of your church. I mean leaders that
we can count on to contest and win elections without
rigging. I am talking about leaders that are fearless and
transparent. I mean leaders with a vision to fight corruption and improve the economy.

Tell me, how do we even win the lost ones over when we don't have any substance to prove our faith? How do we tell them to believe in our God when we have no results to show? As a matter of urgency, we need to stop holding all night prayers asking God to take control. Let me tell you something, God is tired of all those prayers that are inviting Him to come and do for you what you are supposed and capable of doing for yourself.

Right now, start training people to take over the various spheres of the society. Let's make our meetings a breeding ground and a conducive environment for raising leaders and world changers who are not afraid to go out there and make history. Stop joining them to say "we need to pray more." Even if we hold night vigils for a whole year non-stop, God wouldn't come down to change things when you are here. Let your faith push you to produce results.

THIS WILL NOT BE POSSIBLE, NOT WHEN I'M HERE

It was also on record that in those days, Benin City used to be known as the 'City of Blood,' and witchcraft, the occultic and dark powers were very real and widely practiced. So, there was a time they wanted to hold the world witchcraft meeting in Nigeria, and Benin City was chosen to host the meeting.

Idahosa single-handedly came out and publicly made it known that "this will not be possible, not when I'm here." It was all over the media, so the T.V. media decided to hold a meeting with the chief of witchcraft worldwide and Archbishop Idahosa.

They then called on the proposed chief host and told him, Benson Idahosa said, "your world conference of witches cannot hold in Benin City." Responding he said, "Not even God can stop it." He boasted that he was a wizard, and he knew their power.

Our national dailies carried this information on their front pages to the effect that the chief host of Witches and Wizards conference says not even God could stop the conference! The press hurried to Benson Idahosa to report that the chief host had said not even God could stop it.

To their bewilderment, Benson Idahosa said, "the chief host was correct." They said what? Benson Idahosa continued, "God did not need to waste His time stopping witches from coming to Benin City for a conference. That is why I am here. The Lord does not need to consider matters as trivial as that."

The late Archbishop went on air and said there was no way they could hold a meeting where he was, declaring the meeting would not hold. And true to his words, the meeting did not hold. Wow, what a man so full of faith! He said the Lord does not have to consider trivial matters as stopping a conference of witches because he was in that city.

Talk about someone who knew who he was in Christ. Wait a minute! He did not run to the church and call for a night vigil to pray against those witches and wizards. No! I mean there was no casting and binding of all the spiritual forces. And when he heard his pastor say, every Christian has what it takes to raise the dead, he did not lock himself up in a room praying for the dead to come back to life. He went out to see it come to pass.

Where then are the believers of like mind today? Where are the believers who can defy all odds to represent God and His kingdom? We say there is no money in the economy, they run to churches and begin to pray for financial breakthroughs. We say our children are out of school and poverty is everywhere, they say God will take control. And when we see the health sector falling apart, they told us to pray more.

"Destiny is not a matter of chance; it is a matter of choice. It is not a thing to be waited for: it is a thing to be achieved."
William Jennings Bryan

You who are reading this now, I want you to know that you are not a mistake or an afterthought. It is not a mistake that God brought you into this world from that part of the world. It is definitely because He has put the answer to at least one of the myriads of problems facing His people. And my goal with this book is to stir you to action.

"If you are afraid to do it, it cannot be done."
Benson Idahosa

We have become too passive to cause any change for God. We have used prayer as a cover up for too long. And that must stop. We have learnt to become prayer warriors but we've failed to know when to stop praying and carry out God's plan on earth. We have forgotten that prayer is only half of the equation. We are giants and warriors in that corner where we pray but have become timid in the secular world.

It is so sad that this generation of ours don't know when to pray, when not to pray and when to stop praying. It is unfortunate that we don't realize that prayer without works is dead. I beg of you, please do not join those who believe all we need to do is to pray more. When you pray, you need to back it up with prayer inspired actions. That's what your faith is there for. It is there to push you to action.

That's the kind of faith that pushed Benson Idahosa to take action when he heard he could raise the dead. The same faith couldn't allow him to stay behind closed doors praying and binding witches. He went out on air to challenge them. Can God look down today and boldly say, "He doesn't have to come down because you are here?"

IT'S TIME FOR AN ARMY TO ARISE!

Dear reader, I know this for a fact that every local church can be a breeding ground for deliverers. The church is not for entertaining believers, but it is a place to raise up world changers and history makers. Every believer is meant to be what Nehemiah was to Jerusalem.

Every Christian Brother should strive towards becoming what Sir Isaac Newton was to science. All our Christian sisters must identify their area of calling just as Mother Teresa did. Our young men and women should manifest their faith just as Benson Idahosa produce evidence and substance with his faith during his time here on earth. And the pastor's role is to lead them into that Promised Land.

FAITH IS A PUSHER

No room for sitting put again in the body of Christ. It's time for an army of Nehemiahs, Benson Idahosas, Martin Luther Kings to arise and take their place in the nations. This battle is fought using the principles of the kingdom of God to vanquish the kingdom of darkness. It is high time we become more kingdom minded than self-minded my people. Do not resign to fate and inactivity in the guise that we need to pray more.

Brothers and sisters, God is calling for a change. He is calling for a new breed of pastors, religious leaders and ministers to arise. Will you stand in the gap?

"Things do not change; we change."
Henry David Thoreau

In the next chapter, I will be showing you how simple individuals have applied the same model I am sharing with you to bring about tremendous change in their country. Then I will show you how this is applicable to you and me.

It is my conviction that if you apply this principle, while others will be waiting for God to come and save them, you would be making tremendous progress. My dream is to get you up and running dishing out that solution that is inside you for the improvement and development of your community.

NUGGETS

1. Faith is a pusher to go and work. Faith is what does not permit you to sit down and wait for only God knows when.

2. Faith is what energizes you to keep on working, laboring, and searching till you find the missing piece.

3. A person filled with faith is always a workaholic.

4. A man of faith is a man of substance.

5. As Christians, no sector of the economy is allowed to die while we are there.

6. The era of having a church packed full of luke-warm, passive and effortless Christians is over. Let your faith push you to produce results.

7. When you pray, you need to back it up with prayer inspired actions. That's what your faith is there for. It is there to push you to action.

CHAPTER 7
THERE IS A SHORTAGE OF DELIVERERS

From the previous chapter, you saw faith at work. You saw how faith pushed a man to action and he produced results. Faith is a pusher to go and work. Faith is what energizes you to keep on working, laboring, and searching till you find the missing piece. And this was evident in the life of Benson Idahosa.

"If you don't go after what you want, you'll never have it. If you don't ask, the answer is always no. If you don't step forward, you're always in the same place." Nora Roberts

A person filled with faith is always a workaholic. Of a truth, Idahosa was a very energetic and hardworking man. One of the ministers who served under him said that he had never seen a person who worked as hard as Archbishop Benson Idahosa. He was committed and consistent and he has confidence in himself.

Idahosa also spent time studying the works and lives of other successful people both in the gospel ministry and other fields of human endeavors and he applied the principles he learned about these successful people to his life and ministry.

Meanwhile, God needs deliverers like this man to rise up and lead people to victory, using wisdom and power. Earthly forces and authorities only respect visible and tangible force. They will not give in easily.

There is a shortage of deliverers to fix the economy. There are not enough deliverers to fix the political problems. And God is expecting you to become one. God is expecting you to become the deliverer that will fix the ungodliness in entertainment, sports and business. Until you see this, you will miss the heart of God.

I used to see myself as a pastor in Ukraine. But I have changed my job description. I am now the deliverer of a nation. I have identified myself with my country. Her peace is my peace. Her success is my success. Her sins are my sins. Her failures are my failures. And I will share in her salvation too as we transform our country into a model of kingdom principles.

Enough is enough! We cannot continue to try ruling from the sidelines. We must learn to stand up for our nation and the community where we live in. Just as we stand before God in prayers for our personal needs, we too must learn to stand before God for our nation.

"The biggest threats to the church today are fans that call themselves Christians but aren't actually interested in following Christ. They want to be close enough to Jesus to get all the benefits, but not so close that it requires anything from them."
Kyle Idleman

Every one of us should be ready to accept the responsibility that we have a role to play in solving our nations' problems. Once you accept this responsibility, you can no longer be complacent. You will be compelled to innovate and improve and stand against principles of darkness. And then, you can boldly declare as well that God does not need to waste His time coming to take care of trivial matters such as poverty, injustice or illiteracy because you are there. The Lord does not need to consider matters as trivial as that.

Hence, every sector of a nation like the political sector, educational, entertainment, industrial, media, banking and finance, economic, medical, judiciary, housing and every other thing that makes a society thrive will begin to experience life because you are there. The whole earth is waiting for the manifestation of the sons of God.

The whole earth is waiting for deliverers who will arise and emerge to take healing, deliverance, restoration, salvation, and help to the ailing sectors of the economy. The attention right now should be drawn to raising as many deliverers as possible. That is also one of the reasons I wrote this book. And I'm glad you've gone this far with me.

ARE YOU NOT BETTER POSITIONED TO MAKE THE WORLD A BETTER PLACE?

It is rather sad that the most celebrated developments and inventions of the world we live in today were not invented by religious people. In fact, in most cases, they weren't by people who know how to pray all night and fast all day.

Think about the famous Steve Jobs. Did you think he was such a religious person? Do you think he was able to accomplish all he did because he prayed tirelessly? What about the likes of Henry Ford, Thomas Edison, and the Wright Brothers? No, my dear, that was not the case with them.

In fact, some of them have publicly declared that they are atheists. But the truth remains and stands. We can't deny that their lives have made significant impacts in the world today.

A very quick look at some of their contributions will prove that they've played pivotal roles in making the world a better place. It was all thanks to Steve Jobs and Steve Wozniak that computers became affordable for home use when they founded Apple in 1976. Apple II was released a year later in 1977, the world's first mass-market personal computer.

Through their works also, we find ourselves transitioning from the diskettes and floppy disks to the circular, storage devices we are highly familiar with right now – and that is the CD. They also worked on the first Internet-ready computer.

And as we progress, we find our gadgets becoming smaller, handier and easy to carry about. Mobile phones have become not only a highly coveted accessory but also a necessity as well. Take a look at where the iPhone, iPad, and MacBook are presently.

Henry Ford was also responsible for transforming the automobile industry from an invention of unknown utility into an innovation that profoundly shaped the 20th century and continues to affect our live today.

As a matter fact, most of those we celebrate today are out of the church. Bill Gates, Mark Zuckerberg, Thomas Edison, Jack Ma and so on. They are not prayer warriors. But by creating a vacuum inside the electric bulb, finding the right filament to use, and running a low voltage through the bulb, Edison was able to achieve a light bulb that lasted for many hours. Remember that the next time you flip on the switch in your church and prayer houses. And always remember that your computer is produced by another atheist.

Why am I telling you all this? It is to help you see that there is a shortage of deliverers and sons out there that are equipped, trained and empowered to make the world a better place.

Tell me, were these men really the most religious of men? Did they pray better than you do? Were they the ones that went to church the most? Or did you ever read that one of them was a choir master or a departmental leader in their church? Heavens NO!

These were all simple men who realized the enormous potentials available in the human person and decided to explore it to the fullest. They are ordinary men like you and me who dared to take advantage of all that God placed in us as humans and change the world of their day.

So, if without knowing God, they accomplished all these, shouldn't we who know and worship God be able to do much more? Shouldn't we be better positioned to change the world and change our society?

But no, we are too busy praying and doing church. We will rather sit there with folded arms and keep our record as the highest in church attendance for two decades and still counting. My dear friends, it's high time we learned when to stop praying and go to work to make it a better place.

"If science says that it can conceive and build, then faith declares that it can believe and create."
Benson Idahosa

WHERE ARE THE PRAYER WARRIORS OF OUR TIME?

A closer observation of most Hinduism and Buddhist nations in Asia will also prove my point that there is truly a shortage of deliverers in the body of Christ.

China is a good example. Chinese products have flooded markets in Johannesburg, Luanda, Lagos, Cairo, Dakar and other cities, towns, and villages in Africa. Those things include clothing, jewelry, electronics, building materials and much more.

This is because they are very innovative and they put their brilliant minds to work to come up with solutions to the pressing problems and demands. Can you believe that even little things like matches, tea bags, children's toys and bathing soaps are coming from China? In fact, you can still see 'made in China' on some of the plates we use in eating around the continent.

As if that is not enough, it is also disheartening and disgraceful that in the twenty first century, the new headquarters of the African Union (AU), a towering 20-storey building in Addis Ababa, Ethiopia, is so called "China's gift to Africa" because China picked up the $200 million tab for the state-of-the-art complex.

This is an insult and a slap in the face to all Africans that in 2012 a building as significant as the AU headquarters is designed, built and maintained by a foreign company. Yet, we want God to bless us because we pray more.

China had either donated or assisted in building a hospital in Luanda, Angola; a road from Lusaka, Zambia's capital, to Chirundu in the southeast; stadiums in Sierra Leone and Benin; a sugar mill and a sugarcane farm in Mali; and a water supply project in Mauritania, among other projects. Now tell me why God will not bless the works of their hands?

Listen to me; I don't need to be a prophet to tell you this. The people who have taken responsibility to solve the problems in the world will keep getting richer. The companies who construct or repair and maintain the bad roads will definitely get bigger whether you pray or not. The companies who manufacture our basic needs and make it available for us will have an abundance of money irrespective of whether they go to church or not. The earlier we realize this fact, the better for all of us.

Another country worthy of mention here is Taiwan. Taiwan has a great story to tell and many lessons from which developing nations could learn a great deal.

There is a good chance that the phone in your pocket or the laptop in your briefcase was made in Taiwan. Foxconn, the world's largest contract manufacturer according to The Economist and the 43rd biggest company in the world with $117.5 billion in revenues according to Fortune 500 Global rankings, originated from Taiwan. It makes products for companies such as Apple, Cisco, Nokia, Toshiba, Dell, and countless others.

Go check the companies listed on Fortune 500. How many of the top companies listed there did you notice belongs to tongue talking, Holy Ghost filled church goers? How many of them are being run by people who pray a lot or attend religious meetings the most? Where are the prayer warriors of our time?

Why is it that they are not the ones topping the chart? Is it because believers and church faithfuls have become a group of mediocres? No, I personally don't want to believe so.

It is rather unfortunate that our churches and their members haven't been able to match up with the rest of the world because of what I call the deception of religion. Instead of us to get involved with activities that actually result in development and growth, we would rather be locked up in prayer houses and use up our time in churches meetings morning, night and day praying and asking God to take control. In the midst of all that, the rest of the world is moving and making tremendous progress.

BECOME EXCELLENCE MINDED

I'll not fail to talk about Singapore and South Korea. But just before we move on to other countries, it is important to note that in 1962 around the same time most African countries gained independence, Taiwan was a much poorer country with an average annual per capita income of just 170 USD. At the time, this income was on par with Congo, today's poorest nation and paradoxically one of the world's richest in natural resource endowments.

Now in 2017, Taiwan produces and exports electronics, petrochemicals, and machinery and boasts of many branded companies like HTC, Acer, Asus and much more. Taiwan also prides herself as the 19th largest economy in the world by purchasing power parity with only 23 million people. In fact, they've proven that leapfrogging in economic development is possible.

The country has jumped from an Agriculture-based economy in which land was a key resource in the 1950s to an industrial economy in which machines were important in the 1980s to a knowledge-based economy today in which the deep potential of the human mind and ideas matter most.

It is time we inculcate this practice into our society. It is time we began to encourage our students even at a very young age to see opportunities, needs, and problems they can solve. We must encourage production over consumption in our schools and religious organizations. Let each family also start enforcing this attitude at home.

As such, as part of our research of what worked in other places, we should also find out what the best is right now. Research and find out what the record on the ground is and your target should be to beat the best record. For crying out loud, why should we be involved with something and be comfortable doing it lesser than the Europeans or Asians will do it?

I challenge you to get all the necessary training and come up with the best practices. Come up with something that can only be compared to the best in the world. Whatever field or sphere of life you are involved in; only think in terms of the best in the world.

"Desire is the key to motivation, but it's determination and commitment to an unrelenting pursuit of your goal - a commitment to excellence - that will enable you to attain the success you seek."
Mario Andretti

We must become excellence minded and determine to deliver only excellent results. It is time we inculcate excellence in the production of goods and services in our culture and tradition. From here, we can make our locally made products worthy of export.

IT'S TIME TO START USING OUR GENIUSES

This chapter wouldn't be complete if I fail to mention South Korea. Economically, in the 1960s it lagged behind the Democratic Republic of Congo (DRC). However, the interesting thing is that since then, the country's fortunes have diverged spectacularly.

South Korea now belongs to the rich man's club, the OECD Development Assistance Committee (DAC). This clearly shows that countries like South Korea see challenges as obstacles to be overcome, and not as permanent excuses for failure. If not, what else would have transformed her from an agricultural society to an industrialized nation exporting high-technology products such as cars, TVs, mobile phones or computers?

South Korea's chaebols (conglomerates) like Samsung, Hyundai or LG are well known throughout the world. The population of South Korea is also one of the best educated in the world and income in South Korea is distributed very equally compared to the rest of the world.

And talking about Singapore, very few gave tiny Singapore much chance of survival when it was granted independence in 1965. How is it, then, that today the former British colonial trading post is a thriving Asian metropolis with not only the world's number one airline, best airport, and busiest port of trade but also the world's fourth–highest per capita real income?

At its birth Singapore had no natural resources save for its location and its people. But rising from a legacy of divisive colonialism, the devastation of the Second World War, and general poverty and disorder following the withdrawal of foreign forces, Singapore now is hailed as a city of the future.

Just before you get too carried away, it will be very necessary at this point for me to let you know that Singapore was not without problems at inception. The way they responded to these problems is the lesson I want us to learn. They solved their own problems and today, the beauty of the nation speaks for her.

Therefore, if nations like South Korea, Singapore, Japan, China, and Taiwan can become one of the top world economies without any significant natural resources to call their own, then Africa has got no excuse.

In these countries, challenges are often regarded as obstacles to be overcome and not as permanent excuses for failure. This is the new mindset we should all adopt.

My dear friends, the world owes you nothing. Get up on your feet and challenge yourself to solve the problems of your nation. Complains have not and will not solve our problems, instead, tasking our minds to innovatively and creatively solve these problems will.

Singapore made sure that the best and brightest were attracted, that they were paid properly, and they were given full support by their leadership to do their job. Therefore, it's time we all stood up to the challenge before us and brought out the best in us to make our country the hub of progress and development that it was designed to be.

The rest of the world is on a fast lane to development by encouraging research in their learning institutions. It is also very important for us to know that the rest of the world is fast becoming top world economies by engaging their young minds to find solutions to the pressing medical problems and technological challenges.

It is equally important to know that while we are busy with religious activities; other nations around Europe, America, Asia etc., are setting up laboratories and a conducive environment for the next technological and engineering breakthrough.

> *"The price of success is hard work, dedication to the job at hand, and the determination that whether we win or lose, we have applied the best of ourselves to the task at hand."*
> *Vince Lombardi*

Hence, we need to do away with the idea of waiting for God to come and fix our roads, curb corruption, build our schools, create jobs and so on. We must now take the bull by the horn. We must take our national destiny into our hands and chart a course for growth and development in our dear country.

I hope God will look down today and be glad to see that you have started delivering, rebranding and rebuilding various sectors of your nations' economy. I strongly believe that the shortage of deliverers right now will soon become a thing of the past.

NUGGETS

1. Earthly forces and authorities only respect visible and tangible force.

2. I used to see myself as a pastor in Ukraine. But I have changed my job description. I am now the deliverer of a nation.

3. Just as you stand before God in prayers for your personal needs, you must also learn to stand before God for your nation.

4. There is a shortage of deliverers and sons out there that are equipped, trained and empowered to make the world a better place.

5. I don't need to be a prophet to tell you this. The people who have taken responsibility to solve the problems in the world will keep getting richer.

6. Whatever field or sphere of life you are involved in; only think in terms of the best in the world.

7. The world owes you nothing. Get up on your feet and challenge yourself to solve the problems around you.

CHAPTER 8
YOUR FAITH IS PROVEN BY YOUR ACTIONS

"Faith does not suspend our sense of good judgment, it reinforces it." Benson Idahosa

From the previous chapters, it is clearly obvious that prayer is not all a believer needs to make God proud on earth. Prayer is very important, no one can deny that, but it's equally true that prayer is only half of the equation.

The last chapter even made it clearer that God is definitely not against the dignity of labor. If you work out your faith, He'll definitely bless the works of your hands. This was the exact thing we saw in the various examples given in the just concluded chapter.

By now I also want to believe that you clearly understand what prayer truly is. Prayer is actually an on-going, loving relationship and communication with a higher power, which is our heavenly father. Prayer is not just about asking God to help you out in times of need.

The true understanding of prayer comes when you look for God because you want to know him and you establish an on-going relationship with Him - a relationship of trust, love and that of a father to a child. That process of communication that goes on in that relationship is what is called prayer, which could come in form of worship, reading His word or meditation. It could also come in form of a request or a petition.

I'm also confident that you've come to know and understand that God is tired of seeing non-Christians taking advantage of their human potentials to do great things and make the world a better place, while the people who are called by His name are locked up in some buildings on every street crying and shouting in prayers.

I want to also believe that you've come to realize that God is tired of seeing the agnostics and atheists become the real players in all sectors of our nation today, while the Christian brothers and sisters are watching from the sidelines and cheering the unbelievers. We cannot continue to try ruling from the sidelines. We must learn to stand up for our nation and the community where we live in.

The last chapter was primarily about those individuals and nations who have taken advantage of their human potential and confidence in their abilities to make history. It has been about the people who have an eye for problems and come up with an efficient solution even though they don't confess Jesus Christ as the only son of God. It has been about those who activated, unleashed and unlocked the potentials within them to make a difference in their various spheres.

Meanwhile, in this chapter and a couple of chapters following, I'll continue to show you the principles that can transform any passive Christian into an aggressive, passionate and proactive believer, because that is what is lacking in the body of Christ today.

After reading through this chapter, you can never remain nonchalant to kingdom matters. By the time you are done reading this book, it'll become a sin for you to be in a community and people are suffering. You will also know that you have a role to play in nation building.

I can assure you that you will also be aggressively looking for problems to solve. And I can boldly tell you that while others have resorted to praying more, you will take the bull by the horn and start producing tangible results, concrete evidence, and substance that will vindicate your faith and prayers. So, let's continue.

REFUSE TO BE DEFINED
BY YOUR ENVIRONMENT

"You don't drown by falling in water; you drown by staying there." Edwin Louis Cole

What I will be sharing with you in this chapter is about a man who gave true meaning to the above quote. He refused to be defined by the injustice meted on him and his people because he decided to stop praying and start speaking out about the injustice in his environment. I'll like to start by telling you how speaking out in times of injustice can cause a revolution in any environment.

Instead of running behind closed doors to pray, he came out of his prayer closet and spoke about the injustice and inequality in the land and the people of God were delivered. Today, a day has been set apart in America to celebrate a believer and a Christian brother who knew what time to pray, when not to pray and when to stop praying. Today, a group of people can live freely because a man stopped praying and acted upon God's word.

Martin Luther King Jr. was one of America's most influential civil rights activists. His passionate, but nonviolent protests, helped to raise awareness of racial inequalities in America, leading to significant political change. Martin Luther King was also an eloquent orator who captured the imagination and hearts of people, both black and white.

He was born in Atlanta on 15 January 1929. Both his father and grandfather were pastors in an African-American Baptist church. Martin Luther King attended Morehouse College in Atlanta, (segregated schooling) and then went to study at Crozer Theological Seminary in Pennsylvania and Boston University. During his time at University he became aware of the vast inequality and injustice faced by black Americans; in particular

He was influenced by Gandhi's philosophy of non-violent protest. The philosophy of Gandhi tied in with the teachings of his Baptist faith. At the age of 24, King married Coretta Scott, a beautiful and talented young woman. After getting married, King became a priest at Dexter Avenue Baptist Church in Montgomery, Alabama.

Martin Luther King was one of the most prominent advocates of the Civil Rights movement during the 1960s. In contrast to some civil rights activists Martin Luther King generally promoted a non-violent strategy of social change.

A turning point in the life of Martin Luther King was the Montgomery Bus Boycott which he helped to promote. His boycott also became a turning point in the civil rights struggle – attracting national press for the cause.

ARE YOU A FAN OR A PLAYER?

"Fans don't mind him doing a little touch-up work, but Jesus wants complete renovation. Fans come to Jesus thinking tune-up, but Jesus is thinking overhaul. Fans think a little makeup is fine, but Jesus is thinking makeover. Fans think a little decorating is required, but Jesus wants a complete remodel. Fans want Jesus to inspire them, but Jesus wants to interfere with their lives."
Kyle Idleman

A defining moment in the civil rights struggle was to a large degree instigated by Martin Luther King Jr. who was the president of the Montgomery Improvement Association.

Wait a minute! Did I miss something? Do you mean Martin Luther King was a pastor and also the president of a secular organization? Yes! That's exactly what God wants from every one of us. How can we influence our world when we are withdrawn and removed from the challenges facing God's children?

You need to go out there and be part of the solution. There is nothing wrong with our church members leading students union, that's the only way we can ensure and enforce God's principles there. Listen carefully; it is not a sin for a Christian brother to contest an election during the general elections in your state or country. That's the only way the people can rejoice because a righteous man is ruling. We need believers in the senate and House of Representatives as well to make laws that will favor God's course.

We are only observing from the sidelines because we've decided to remain fans and never a player. The Christians who should be in the seat of power are busy praying, while the unbelievers are looting the economy and impoverishing the masses. And all we do is to keep praying that God will remove them from office. But whenever I hear such prayer requests, I begin to ask myself, if God should answer this prayer and the unbelievers are out of office, where are the believers to take over from them?

My dear friends, it's time to begin raising up leaders like Martin Luther King and the likes of Benson Idahosa in our nation. It's time we learn from the examples of the patriarchs of faith and stop being religious about prayers. We need to stop praying and start acting. There is a time to pray and there is also a time to stop praying or not pray at all.

Yes, I mean there is a time you should NOT pray at all. David was not praying when he killed Goliath. He was acting on God's word at that moment. He had been fellowshipping with God in the wilderness, while he was pasturing his father's sheep. So, when Goliath began challenging Israel, it was not a time to run to the top of the mountain and start praying. It was a time to act! So, don't come with all your religious arguments here.

You remember the story of Nehemiah earlier in this book? When Sanbalat, Tobiah, and all their allies came to attack them, what did they do? Of course, they prepared for battle because it was not a time to keep pray-ing. The time to fight has come and they prepared to fight. You will recall that Nehemiah and the Israelites worked with a trowel in one hand and sword in the oth-er. Half were prepared for war while half continued the work of strengthening the walls that were necessary for the protection of Jerusalem.

They were so convinced that nothing can stop the re-building of the wall. That is faith at work there. Faith is not some senseless, illogical theories you always hear ev-ery day from different preachers. Faith is an action word. Faith produces result. Faith is the substance of things hoped for and the evidence of things not seen.

When you ask King David today, where is the evi-dence of your faith? He will confidently show you the head of Goliath. And if you also ask Nehemiah, where is the substance your faith and prayers produced? He will point to the walls of Jerusalem.

Dear reader, there is a time to hold night vigils, but also remember that there is a time to stay awake and plan or strategize on the way forward for our nation. And such times are here already. We have prayed for too long and locked ourselves up in prayer houses but I'm here to tell you that God is not deaf. He hears your prayers. So, let's begin to act on His word and rebuild our nation.

The time to release a blueprint on how to take our children who are out of school, and take them back to school is here. The time to take those kids hawking on the streets to survive is now. The time to liberate our government from the chains of corruption is here. The time to cure cancer eating up our economy and hard labor is not tomorrow but now. So, roll up your sleeves and get to work.

THE TURNING POINT

"The question here is not whether we will face uncomfortable situations, but how we will respond in these situations."
Jeff Shore

The turning point in the civil rights struggle all began in innocuous circumstances on 5th December 1955. Rosa Parks, a civil rights activist, refused to give up her seat – she was sitting in a white only area. This broke the strict segregation of colored and white people on the Montgomery buses.

The bus company refused to back down and so Martin Luther King helped to organize a strike where colored people refused to use any of the city buses. The boycott lasted for several months; the issue was then brought to the Supreme Court who declared the segregation was unconstitutional.

My dear brothers and sisters, what problems have you decided to resolve with your life? What solutions will you devote your life to? What problem will you be known to have resolved? What problem will cease to exist because you pass through this world? Will you be the voice for the voiceless? Can people look to you and find hope because of the ideals you stand for?

After the success of the Montgomery bus boycott, King and other ministers founded the Southern Christian Leadership Conference (SCLC). This proved to be a nucleus for the growing civil rights movement.

Martin Luther King was an inspirational and influential speaker; he had the capacity to move and uplift his audiences. In particular, he could offer a vision of hope. He captured the injustice of the time but also felt that this injustice was like a passing cloud. King frequently made references to God, the Bible, and his Christian Faith.

His speeches were largely free of revenge, instead focusing on the need to move forward. He was named as Man of the Year by Time magazine in 1963, it followed his famous and iconic "I have a dream Speech" – delivered in Washington during a civil rights march.

> *"I have a dream that one day this nation will rise up and live out the true meaning of its creed: "We hold these truths to be self-evident: that all men are created equal." I have a dream that one day on the red hills of Georgia the sons of former slaves and the sons of former slave owners will be able to sit down together at a table of brotherhood"*
> *Martin Luther King*

The following year, Martin Luther King was awarded the Nobel Peace Prize for his work towards social justice. At the age of thirty-five, Martin Luther King, Jr., was the youngest man to have received the Nobel Peace Prize (1964). King announced he would turn over the prize money $54,123 to the civil rights movement. In his honor, America has instigated a national Martin Luther King Day.

He remains symbolic of America's fight for justice and racial equality. To this day, King remains a potent symbol of the African American civil rights movement. His speeches offer a striking exposition of some of the ideals of the civil rights movement.

Just before we move on, let me quickly tell you a little about another individual who served as a symbol of hope for her people.

THE COURAGEOUS QUEEN ESTHER

The book of Esther is one of only two books in the entire Bible named for women. Esther contains the story of a beautiful young Jewess who risked her life to serve God and save her people.

Esther lived in ancient Persia about 100 years after the Babylonian captivity. When Esther's parents died, the orphaned child was adopted and raised by her older cousin, Mordecai.

One day the king of the Persian Empire, Xerxes I, threw a lavish party. On the final day of the festivities, he called for his queen, Vashti, eager to flaunt her beauty to his guests. But the queen refused to appear before Xerxes. Filled with anger, he deposed Queen Vashti, forever removing her from his presence.

To find his new queen, Xerxes hosted a royal beauty pageant and Esther was chosen for the throne. Her cousin Mordecai became a minor official in the Persian government of Susa.

Soon after, Mordecai uncovered a plot to assassinate the king. He told Esther about the conspiracy, and she reported it to Xerxes, giving credit to Mordecai. The plot was thwarted and Mordecai's act of kindness was preserved in the chronicles of the king.

At this same time, the king's highest official was a wicked man named Haman. He hated the Jews and he especially hated Mordecai, who had refused to bow down to him.

So, Haman devised a scheme to have every Jew in Persia killed. The king bought into the plot and agreed to annihilate the Jewish people on a specific day. Meanwhile, Mordecai learned of the plan and shared it with Esther, challenging her with these famous words:

> *"Do not think that because you are in the king's house you alone of all the Jews will escape. For if you remain silent at this time, relief and deliverance for the Jews will arise from another place, but you and your father's family will perish. And who knows but that you have come to your royal position for such a time as this?"*

Esther 4:13-14 (NIV)

When I read this story again recently, I pictured the present day believers. If you read the first part of the above scripture carefully and attentively, you will agree with me that a lot of believers nowadays think their prayers will help them escape the evil in the society. Hence, they've remained silent and resorted to praying in their closet.

But let's take a closer look at how she responded to this issue. The Jewish exile Mordecai knew the situation was dire and dangerous. Esther and Mordecai knew that to come before the king without a formal invitation, even though Esther was the queen, could mean she would be put to death.

Esther urged all of the Jews to fast and pray for deliverance. Then risking her own life, she acted on her faith. The brave young Esther approached the king with a plan of her own.

She invited Xerxes and Haman to a banquet where eventually she revealed her Jewish heritage to the king, as well as Haman's diabolical plot to have her and her people killed. In a rage, the king ordered Haman to be hung on the gallows - the very same gallows Haman had built for Mordecai.

Mordecai was promoted to Haman's high position and Jews were granted protection throughout the land. As the people celebrated God's tremendous deliverance, the joyous festival of Purim was instituted.

YOU ARE HERE FOR
SUCH A TIME AS THIS

You must have noticed a trend throughout this chapter. They all stood for a problem. They stood for a cause. They prayed and they put their faith to work even though they risked their lives in the process. They were the 'Nehemiahs,' to their generations.

Dear reader, the world is in need of men and women like this, who are not afraid of problems. The world is in desperate need of problem solvers. Your nation desperately needs you to solve the problems in the land. And who knows, maybe you are here for such a time as this? Just like Mordecai challenged Esther.

When a man of faith believes God for anything, he also goes ahead to do everything necessary to produce the result. This was exactly what Martin Luther King, Nehemiah, Benson Idahosa and Esther did.

The substance of those things you've prayed or hoped for is your affirmations. They are your credentials. Your substance is your vindication. Your substance will vindicate you. Your substance should vindicate your prayer. Your substance validates your faith and it should validate your prayers as well.

Substances are not produced without doing something. Substances don't come out of wishful thinking. Substances don't respond to desires. So, if you truly believe you are a man or woman of faith; if you really believe God, then faith becomes a pusher on your inside.

That faith will never allow you to sit in one place anymore. That faith pushes you to arise and do everything necessary to produce the substance that corresponds with what you've been believing God for. The substance should correspond with what you've been believing that you can do. The substance should correspond with what you've been praying for or even more.

You are here for such a time as this. Therefore, go out today and put your faith to work!

NUGGETS

1. If you work out your faith, God will definitely bless the works of your hands.

2. There is nothing wrong with our church members leading students union, that's the only way we can ensure and enforce God's principles there. It is not a sin for a Christian brother to contest an election during the general elections in your state or country. That's the only way the people can rejoice because a righteous man is ruling.

3. The Christians who should be in the seat of power are busy praying, while the unbelievers are looting the economy and impoverishing the masses.

4. The world is in desperate need of problem solvers.

5. There is a time to hold night vigils, but also remember that there is a time to stay awake and plan or strategize on the way forward for our nation.

6. When a man of faith believes God for anything, he also goes ahead to do everything necessary to produce the result.

7. You are here for such a time as this. Therefore, go out today and put your faith to work!

CHAPTER 9
WHEN NOT TO PRAY!

L ike I mentioned briefly in the last chapter, using
the story of David and Goliath as an example,
there is a time you should NOT pray at all. And I'll elaborate more on it here. David was only acting on God's
word at that moment when he came face to face with
Goliath.

You don't go to the battlefield preparing for war or
unprepared. You either go prepared or you never come
back alive. So, when Goliath began challenging Israel, it
was not a time to run to the mountain top to pray or call
together the prayer warriors to start interceding. It was
a time to act!

One of our favorite Bible stories as children is the story of David and Goliath from 1 Samuel 17. Children love
this story since the hero is a young boy not much older
than those hearing the story told in Sunday school class.
But the story of David and Goliath is not just for children. It is a fascinating story that never gets old to read.

The chapter opens as Israel and the Philistines are
facing off in battle. David's older brothers were with
the army of Israel while David was at home tending the
sheep. David's father, Jesse, sent him to the war zone
to deliver some food to his brothers and find out news
about the war. David quickly arranged for others to take
care of the sheep while he took off for the battlefront.

RIGHTEOUS ANGER

David arrived at the battlefield to find his brothers and the rest of the Israeli army cowering in fear from the taunts of Goliath of Gath. Goliath was the champion of the Philistine army. Though he was about 9 feet tall, he spoke words that angered David.

Goliath was claiming the God of the Israelites was not able to help them in battle. Whatever fear David may have had, it was secondary to the righteous indignation he had for the words of the giant. Goliath had blasphemed David's God and David aimed to stand up for what was right.

Before you read on, don't you think there are a lot of things happening around us today that should activate a righteous anger in you? Don't you think poverty in Africa has made our God look like a pauper that cannot take care of His children? Don't you think injustice should activate a holy anger in you?

A righteous anger should always come from within you whenever you see our bad roads. How can you see our young graduates out of school without jobs and not be angered? How on earth can you live in an environment where the health facilities and teaching materials for schools are inadequate and you are not angered?

For goodness sake, how can you go to work every day and see young children who should be in school hawking on the streets and you are not even moved? How can those of us who have been told that we are the salt of the earth neglect our roles all in the name of prayer?

Can you just imagine what a country we will have if all the 80 million believers in Nigeria will be angered by the injustices in our society? Think how many problems facing our country today will find it impossible to grow because the righteous anger in us has pushed us to tackle each of these problems? Think how many problems facing your country today will be inhibited just by being proactive?

Believers who should have been trained and taught to go into the various sectors of the country and be pushed to act in such areas have been restricted to the four walls of a church. They have been taught that all that matters is attendance to church services while the environment where the service hold stay in absolute darkness and the street outside the church is littered with beggars and old men and women without homes to live in.

The church is supposed to be the catalyst for the growth that we all wish and pray for. The church and its members are supposed to bring about the healthy society we are dreaming about. But all these will never happen if we don't step out of our comfort zones. All these will never happen if we only kneel and pray all day waiting for God.

Dear reader, God is calling for a change right now. My dear sister, God is calling for a change that will begin with you. He is asking that you begin to use your faith to produce results. We must begin to show evidence for all those hours of prayers. You must realize that the reason things have remained the way they are is because you haven't been involved with the system.

Right now, we must begin to do away with the fear of being involved with the politics of the land. We must re-educate our young and promising leaders against the idea that politics is a dirty game that should be played by the dirty. They must understand that if politics is dirty, then, it's their responsibility to clean it up. This is the way we can begin to employ the energy from that righteous anger into good use.

PREPARE TO FIGHT

As we go on with the story of David and Goliath, I want you to be very attentive to every step he took. I want you to note that he was ready to fight Goliath. He did not even have a special prayer session just before he challenged Goliath openly.

Ignoring the potential danger, David trusted in God to help him fight Goliath. David said that he would fight the giant. Please note, he did not say he needs to pray more.

He was immediately taken before King Saul. Though he was a young man, he had experienced enough danger in his life to know God was in control and would protect him through the battle. David told Saul as much and Saul offered David the royal armor.

Whether David felt unworthy or unwieldy using Saul's armor, he refused to accept the kind and generous offer. More than likely David simply trusted in the God he knew than in the armor he did not know.

After leaving Saul, David ran towards Goliath prepared to fight. He gathered 5 smooth stones from the river and pocketed 4 of them. The 5th one went into the sling prepared for Goliath. They ran towards one another.

Goliath mocked David and said that he was not afraid of a little boy. David said that the Philistine came with a sword, shield, and spear, but David came with confidence in the God of Israel. David boldly replied that he had no fear of Goliath and that the birds would be picking the flesh off his giant body by the end of the day.

David let fly the stone in his sling. The stone hit the giant between the eyes and the stone sunk into his forehead. Goliath fell forward while both armies watched. David then pulled the giant sword from its sheath and chopped off the head of the Philistine champion.

David returned to King Saul with the head of Goliath. In the meantime, the army of the Philistines retreated as quickly as they could. Their champion was dead and they apparently were ill prepared to face the army of God. The Israelites chased the Philistines and won the victory that day. When they returned to the empty Philistine camp they took the treasures they could find.

ARE YOU A DECEIVER
OR A BELIEVER?

David trusted more in God than in weapons of war. He knew that his battle was on behalf of the living God of Israel. Interestingly, David fought for God when it was appropriate but he did not try to take the throne from Saul. He let God fight the battles for him. David fought for causes, not personal agenda.

While we don't fight physical giants today, we do fight corruption, injustice, illiteracy, economy melt down, wrong doctrines in the church and other vices. It was on record that David ran towards Goliath; will you run towards the problem in your sphere of expertise to proffer solutions? Will you avail yourself to be used as an instrument of national transformation and deliverance?

By fighting for the poor, you are fighting for God. By being a voice to the voiceless and hope to the hopeless, you do that unto God. David fought for God. You can also fight for God when you take responsibility to solve problems that leave God's children helpless, beggarly and hopeless.

David manifested raw faith. Faith is what makes you go all out. Faith is what makes you persevere and keep on going till you get the result. Faith is what makes you keep on believing and keep on fighting. Faith is what makes you keep on standing when nobody else believes you because you believe, you know you can do it, you know it'll work. That is faith and that's what you do in prayer.

So, you don't just pray. You know when to stand up from that place of prayer and go work to create and produce the substance. You don't just pray and sit still waiting for angels to bring the result down supernaturally. You don't just pray and wait for the government to get the job done or someone else. If that's all you do, to just pray and expect someone else or some supernatural intervention to get the job done, then you are a deceiver, not a believer.

Your faith is proved by your actions. It is your faith that encourages you. Your faith lifts you up from your seat. Your faith lifts you up from your bed and pushes you to go and create. Faith, therefore, is a force of creation. It is the faith that God had that made Him leave the heavens to create the earth.

Your faith gives you the confidence and strength to go after whatsoever you believe in. Your faith gets you up from that bed and gives you so much energy and so much encouragement, so much that you don't need any external encouragement again. That's faith at work.

"Faith in God is the most dynamic force in humanity." Benson Idahosa

If you actually pray, it will make you stand up and go to work on your prayer points. When everybody is giving up, you are still working. Prayer is a force of creation as well. Your faith makes you to be so sure and so certain of what you are praying about. When you believe God in prayer, that faith in prayer makes you to be so sure and so full of confidence that it pushes you to go and produce the result.

When you really believe in prayer, you know that nothing can stop you from going to get what you need. When you believe, you just know that nothing can stop this thing. The substance must be produced.

A man of faith does not stop in his quest until he has seen the substance of what he believes God for, or what he is praying for. You will pursue it until you have produced the result. So, the product or element of what you believe God for or pray for is the proof of your faith.

If you need to push, push. If you need to fight, fight. If you need to work, work until you get it. The purpose of faith, therefore, is to inspire you to action. Faith comes to inspire you. Faith comes to kick you out of your comfort zone. Faith causes you to stand up and not to be weary. So also is prayer.

YOU ARE A DELIVERER!

Many years ago, there was a problem in Egypt. Nobody could give an answer to the problem but Joseph did. That was how a slave boy, turned prisoner and later a prime minister, was able to deliver a whole nation from an impending economic doom. How much more you with all your education and training?

Joseph's brothers conspired against him and sold him to some Ishmaelite traders. The Ishmaelite traders, in turn, sold him as a slave to Potiphar, a wealthy Egyptian merchant. Joseph found great fortune with Potiphar, but his promotion through Potiphar's household attracts the attention of Potiphar's wife, who repeatedly tried to seduce him. When her attempts failed, she accused Joseph of rape, which landed him in prison.

Though now in the deepest of his life's trenches, God was still with Joseph. His fellow inmates, Pharaoh's former butler, and his former baker, both dreamt symbolic dreams, and Joseph's skills as a dream-interpreter were put to use. He predicted that the butler will be exonerated in three days and restored to Pharaoh's service and that the baker will be put to death. Joseph's interpretations came true.

Joseph asks the butler to remember him once he's back in Pharaoh's service, but the butler did not fulfill his promise until Pharaoh himself had a series of disturbing dreams two full years later. These dreams prove to be Joseph's ultimate turn of good luck.

"When you begin to worry, go find something to do. Get busy being a blessing to someone; do something fruitful. Talking about your problem or sitting alone, thinking about it, does no good; it serves only to make you miserable. Above all else, remember that worrying is totally useless. Worrying will not solve your problem." Joyce Meyer

He was brought to the court to interpret two famous dreams of Pharaoh: one in which seven sickly cows consume seven healthy cows, and a parallel dream in which seven sickly ears of grain consume seven lush ears of grain.

Joseph told Pharaoh: *"Seven years are coming, a great abundance through the land. Then seven years of famine will arise."* With this knowledge in hand, Pharaoh prepares Egypt for famine. And Joseph, at the age of 30, was appointed second-in-command to Pharaoh.

If one man who was taken away from his family into slavery could come up with solutions that sustained a whole nation and other neighboring countries during one of the worst famines in bible times, think of what is possible if every person reading this will go back to the secular world and begin to solve pressing problems.

This goes to show you how relevant each one of us is in the transformation of your society if we woke up. This also shows how much we are depriving our nation of by our insensitivity and selfishness demonstrated in the way we do church today.

My dear friend, look for problems and once you identify the problems, begin to provide solutions. Once you see the problems, come up with your suggestions. Research on how best the problem can be resolved. Come up with calculated results. Come up with answers. You are a deliverer of nations.

THE POWER HIDDEN IN RESOLVING PROBLEMS

The famine that Joseph predicted ultimately brought the sons of Jacob to Egypt. With no other options, and hearing of excess grain in the neighboring country, Jacob's sons made a series of trips down to Egypt. Upon discovering his brothers some 20 years after selling him into slavery, Joseph concealed his identity and tested his family, locking up his brother Simeon until the rest of his brothers return with Benjamin.

Jacob was reluctant to send Benjamin - his last child of Rachel - but he ultimately relented. Only upon seeing Benjamin did Joseph revealed himself to his brothers, granted them forgiveness, and brought the entire family down to Egypt. Joseph died in Egypt at the age of 110.

You will notice here that Joseph's brothers came to Egypt to buy grains. That ultimately indicates that the solution proposed by Joseph also helped in sustaining other neighboring countries.

The problem Joseph solved for Pharaoh also brought Egypt a fortune as one of the only countries in the world during that famine that had enough to eat and to sell to other nations. The solution to the famine made Egypt the economic power. This is the potential hidden in finding solutions to problems.

"Inside of every problem lies an opportunity."
Robert Kiyosaki

I can boldly tell you that the solution to the hunger and poverty in Nigeria could be the only thing the continent of Africa has been waiting for. If Egypt could turn a supposed problem – 'Famine' into a fortune, why can't Africa turn the hunger in the continent around in her favor to be a provider of food for the world?

The solution to the numerous problems in Africa to-day could make her the leading continent tomorrow. These problems are waiting for you to solve them and make the world a better for all of us. Are you still waiting around?

While a lot of people are complaining of lack of job opportunities in their indigenous countries, here comes Joseph, second-in-command in a foreign land in charge of their economic policies. That is a glaring model of the power hidden in resolving problems.

That job you've been praying for might just be an idea away from you. Who knows if that financial break-through you've been fasting for is just waiting for the solution locked up inside you? Go out there and make a difference. Different sectors of your country are waiting for deliverers.

All you have to do is first look and see what God wants to be done, and then do what God wants to be done with the gifts that God has given you and the experiences He has allowed in your life. If you will faithfully do that, the abundance of God will pour into your life. Life is not about earning a living. It is far more than that. Just look at the birds, the plants, and all of nature's creations around you. Birds don't earn a living.

Birds and God's other creatures simply do what they were sent here to do. If you will simply trust in God and do what you were sent here to do which is to solve problems and be a solution provider wherever you find yourself, then, God's abundance will be with you forever.

If only you will be proactive today about the problems around you, and stop using prayer as a cover up, you will discover that every problem has its solution within it like the hole in Goliath's armor. Every problem no matter how big and insurmountable it may appear to be had within it, its weakness and that's where the solution to the problem lies.

In the next chapter, I'll be sharing with you the three most important ingredients every believer must and should always possess at all time. You will also get a better understanding of the times so that you can effortlessly know where to draw the lines talking about when to pray, when not to pray and when to stop praying.

NUGGETS

1. You don't go to the battlefield preparing for war or unprepared. You either go prepared or you never come back alive.

2. The church is supposed to be the catalyst for the growth that we all wish and pray for. But it will never happen if we don't step out of our comfort zones.

3. If politics is dirty, then, it's your responsibility to clean it up.

4. By fighting for the poor, you are fighting for God. By being a voice to the voiceless and hope to the hopeless, you do that unto God.

5. Faith is what makes you persevere and keep on going till you get the result.

6. Prayer is a force of creation.

7. If only you will be proactive today about the problems around you, and stop using prayer as a cover up, you will discover that every problem has its solution within it like the hole in Goliath's armor.

CHAPTER 10
PRAYER, FAITH AND HARD WORK ARE INTERTWINED

By now, I believe you already have a fair idea of what prayer, faith, and hard work really is. In this chapter, you will come to understand that these three concepts are inseparable. They are intertwined. There is no way you tell me you want to pray without faith. And there is certainly no way that prayer can be effective without you working it out. This is where I'll like to pitch my tent in this chapter.

I am a firm believer in praying. But I also know that a lot of Christians don't know that there is a time to pray, a time not to pray and a time to stop praying. A believer must be able to differentiate between all these.

If there is anything I could choose to be a hallmark of my life, it is prayer. It was said about Jesus that He prayed a lot. I too have endeavored to live my life through prayer. I have disciplined myself at times to spend weeks in prayer, interrupted only by sleep. Those times have changed my life. They are spent absorbing His presence, His glory, and His strength.

I have never prayed for the sake of praying. I have prayed because I want to be with God, to get to know Him, and then to radiate His glory. To me, this is the point of my life.

Nevertheless, prayer without work is dead. Also, action without prayer is foolish. Even if your intentions are good, even if you are trying to build God's kingdom, you cannot succeed without prayer. But prayer is not an end in itself.

Prayer is not merely a habit but a way of life. We can commune constantly with God. Learn to lay your soul bare before God. Learn to humble yourself before Him in prayer. Learn to admit your weaknesses and your mistakes in His presence.

Put your trust in Him. He is your hope, your source, your life. All else could fail, but having Him, you have everything. Let Him know that you are trusting completely in Him. Fast so as to humble your flesh.

Learn also to wait on the Lord. It's important not just to storm the heavens with your prayers, but to rest in God and to be guided by His assessment of the situation, relying on Him in everything.

God always gives grace to the person who humbles himself before Him and who sets his hopes on Him. No matter what defeats that person may suffer, God makes it possible for him to spread his wings and mount up on new heights. God will equip him supernaturally and show him how to remain standing even when others fall.

In prayer, you learn who God is and what He wants you to do. The revelations you receive in the place of prayer are like foundation stones upon which you can build your life, family, and calling according to God's plan.

The revelations you receive in prayer will unveil the prototype or picture of what you should do next. If you put these revelations into action according to His model, you will walk a well-trodden pathway and not just go around in circles.

If you receive a word of revelation and have an understanding of what God wants to build and the unique way in which He is going to bring what He has in mind to pass; if you take the steps He is expecting you to take, then your life and calling become light. You will find pleasure and great delight in them.

It's no longer you who is building, but God. He goes before you, accomplishing the things He has called and appointed you for. You have only to be an obedient doer of His will. Take note of the word 'doer.' The things you build in the here and now will have already been built in heaven, and you will simply be establishing them.

SO, IT'S TIME TO STOP PRAYING

Many are afraid of the consequences of taking risks. They don't want to feel pain. This fear, like all fear, is rooted in egocentrism. And that's the primary reason most Christians nowadays are so much crazy about miracles. They have been eaten up deep by the evil of instant gratification.

When you are not dead to yourself, you fear the consequences of failure. Egocentrism masquerades as humility and practical thinking. But it's focused on yourself and what causes you pain. That's called serving your own comfort. You are not looking out for kingdom interests but your own.

True humility goes where God leads, regardless of the consequences. It recognizes that we are dead to ourselves but alive in Christ. We don't live our own lives anymore. We were headed for hell when He rescued us. So we don't call the shots anymore; He does. His will is our command, no matter if it brings us life or death.

You have been given your promised land so that you can fight and take it victoriously. If you have a calling from the lord and do nothing to fulfill it, you are on the verge of being ruined. It is not your work but God's. He has entrusted you with it. If you have been working with too little for too long, then you probably haven't been faithful.

By definition, if you are faithful with little, you will graduate to much. Nobody is supposed to muddle around with little things his whole life. You were made for greatness and big things.

With an approximate overall 400 million Christians in Africa, millions are still flooding to join Pentecostal churches in Africa where vows of miraculous healing and promises of pending fortunes attract the overwhelming population of sick and poor on the continent.

In particular, the West African nation of Nigeria is experiencing the fastest growth in Christianity on the continent with Pentecostal churches playing a large role in this development.

But what makes Nigeria as well as many other African nations unique is their heavy emphasis on instant gratification and miracles, which incorporate traditional African beliefs and material blessings.

Meanwhile, Pentecostal Christianity has increased along with poverty in Nigeria during the last couple of decades. And our messages of instant gratification have created a generation of people who only want to see instant results, immediate relief, and a painless effort. This is not the natural course of nature or a better way of doing things.

Instead of messages that only promise blessings, miracles, breakthroughs, and wonders, let us replace these messages with preaching on virtues such as hard work, creativity, dedication, commitment, perseverance, diligence, and responsibility. These things will produce a responsible society.

The same bible you read every day says, *"by the labor of your hand, you shall eat; happiness and prosperity will be yours."* (Psalm 128:2) Therefore, prosperity, breakthroughs will never emanate from idleness and laziness. This gullibility must change and it must stem from our pulpits. We must show our hearers the proper way to wealth.

Let us start immediately by using correct words of encouragement by telling them to work hard and stop relying solely on prayer as the only way to get relieved from their pains. God instituted work in the beginning. So, let's stop looking at work as a form of curse or punishment. Just as faith without work is dead, so also is prayer without work is equally dead.

PUT YOUR CREATIVE
ABILITIES TO WORK

When you read in the book of beginnings, right there in the first chapter, the bible elaborates on the process of creation from day one up until the seventh say on which God rested. We were told how that the lights were created. The firmaments after and then the waters were separated from the earth.

As soon as the earth (dry land) emerged, it was commanded to bring forth grass, the herb yielding seed, and the fruit tree yielding fruit after his kind, whose seed is in itself, upon the earth: and it was so. By the end of the fifth day, everything necessary for life on earth had been made. Then on the sixth day, God created His ultimate creature – man!

Just as He was about to do that though, God made it clear that the man He wanted to create was one that would be in His image and likeness. This means that man was created to look like God and to function like God.

Asides from telling us the reason for man and his features, as soon as man was created, God went on to elaborate on what he was created to do. God said he should be fruitful, productive, multiply, and replenish the earth. He also added that man should subdue the earth, that is to bring under control and to have dominion, which is to reign over the fish of the sea, the fowl of the air and over everything that moves upon the earth.

Man was placed on earth to have dominion over all the three realms of existence in the earth. This is why God never had to invent the airplane, man did. God never had to invent a ship to move on the sea, man did. God didn't create cars and all the other vehicles that move on land, man did as well!

These are not things that necessarily require more prayers to activate the creative power within us. That's why unbelievers who don't even pray as much as we do, that's if they pray at all, can conveniently make up the majority of those inventing those stuff. Talk of the Wright brothers and Henry Ford.

Friends, it is high time we stopped behaving like the creative ability of God was removed from Africans before they were born. We should stop acting like when God blessed man and said he should be fruitful, he exempted Africans. Why are we acting as though, we need to beg God to give us what He already put in us before we were born?

How disheartening it is to know that someone has described our dear nation as a nation orchestrated to administrate and not to produce. Everyone is thinking of how to get elected into power so they can "be in control." Our country is full of so called engineers who only want to stay in air-conditioned offices. Youths no longer want to go to technical schools because it is now assumed to be less prestigious!

No one is thinking what they can do or produce for the benefit of the country yet, we have about 180 million people in whom God has placed His creative ability all living within the same country! And we have the courage to say the only solution to our problems is to 'pray more.' What a shame!

WHERE IS THE EVIDENCE
OF YOUR FAITH?

I can boldly tell you that sometimes people in the world who don't know the Lord Jesus Christ or even read the bible have more confidence in their creative abilities than some of us who just sit in the pews or churches claiming that we are believers but we don't have anything to show for it.

People like Bill Gates; he has so much faith in himself. He left Harvard. Harvard is everyone's dream. Everyone

143

wants to get a certificate from Harvard. But he had more faith in himself than what Harvard will offer him. He had so much substance on his inside that he left the university to go produce the evidence of his faith in himself. He left the university to go produce the substance of what he had believed in.

Faith in himself made him leave that university. And now he's been invited to lecture at the same university where he dropped out many years ago. Faith will never allow you to be idle. You want to tell me that all those religious activities that keep people in church all day, praying and refusing to do any other thing and you have nothing to show for it, is called faith? Is that what you are telling me? Come on, definitely, that cannot be regarded as faith, my brother.

> *"If you have no confidence in self, you are twice defeated in the race of life."*
> *Marcus Garvey*

Faith is what will make you so much believe in what you are praying for that you cannot sit down again. Faith is what will push you to go out and produce results. Faith is that energy that makes you to be so sure and work with all you've got to get the result because you so much believe the result is out there. You so much believe you are capable of producing that result.

Faith always produces substance. So also is prayer. Prayer must have substance. If there is no substance to back it up, then it's dead. Prayer without work is dead.

Your faith can only be proven by your substance. Your faith must be vindicated by the substance you produce.

Your prayers must have results and evidence. A man of prayer is a man of substance. Just like the patriarchs of faith.

The patriarchs of our faith were men and women of substance. Jesus is a man of substance. He built the biggest faith movement, the biggest religion in the world. He had the highest number of followers in the world. Even in His time, He produced substance all the time. He had results, and not just miracles signs and wonders. Paul was also a man of substance. So, dear believers, where is your substance? Where is the evidence of your faith?

WHAT DIFFERENTIATES THE HIGH ACHIEVERS OF TODAY FROM OTHERS?

Do you know that Bill Gates' first business failed? Yes, the richest person in the whole world couldn't make any money at first. Yet, that couldn't stop a man that is obsessed with getting what he believed in.

Bill Gates' first company, Traf-O-Data (a device which could read traffic tapes and process the data), failed miserably. When Gates and his partner, Paul Allen, tried to sell it, the product wouldn't even work. Gates and Allen didn't let that stop them from trying again though.

Here's how Allen explained how the failure helped them: *"Even though Traf-O-Data wasn't a roaring success, it was seminal in preparing us to make Microsoft's first product a couple of years later."*

"It had long since come to my attention that people of accomplishment rarely sat back and let things happen to them. They went out and happened to things." Leonardo da Vinci

I believe by now, that it's becoming obvious to you that what differentiates the high achievers of today from others is their choice to stay awake and see their dreams come true. Their choice to recognize that no one owes them anything and taking responsibility for their lives was a determining factor in their success stories.

Here you are crying and complaining about your lack of education for how your life has turned out. Maybe I need to remind you here that Bill Gates did not graduate from college. Or Benjamin Franklin, one of the prominent founding fathers of America couldn't afford his education, but through self-education, they made their dreams possible.

"The road to your success is not a highway. You have to create it as you go"
Bangambiki Habyarimana

Benjamin Franklin's parents couldn't afford his education but he continued learning. He taught himself through voracious reading. Have you ever looked around to see what you can teach yourself that could make a difference in your life?

Have you ever thought of what you could do with your free time that will make your life better? What can you do today that will improve you mentally, physically, or financially? What books can you read that will make you a better leader? Therein lays the key to your greatness.

Bill Gates dropped out of college but taught himself how to code properly. He dropped out of 'formal education' but not out of 'self-education.' He improved on his coding skills by constantly practicing and staying for hours with his computer. This was his key to a life of prominence.

Even when he failed at his first business venture, the discipline he already developed to teach himself by practicing and spending the time to perfect his coding skills couldn't allow that singular failed attempt to define his future. He continued to improve and he is the richest man today because he was willing to do what most losers won't. What he lacked in formal education, he made up for it in self-education.

A very good population in the world now has access to the Internet. Do you know that you can teach yourself to become a better cook by watching the right videos on YouTube? Do you know that you can teach yourself almost anything with the bank of information on line? There are lots of information available for free on line.

Dear reader, be your own teacher. Educate yourself. Starting from today; read those books that will make you a better fashion designer. Don't wait till you have the money to pay for a college degree. Teach yourself how to play those musical instruments. Invest your time on it.

The more time you spend practicing the better you become. You don't necessarily need to have thousands of dollars to pay an expert to teach you. Start from where you are, with what you have, to teach yourself. This will make your heavenly father proud of you because you have started putting His creative ability in you to work.

In the next chapter, you will be reading about some of the evils of instant gratification and how it has enslaved and imprisoned Christians. You will also see what you can start doing immediately after praying.

I'm sure you already know that instant gratification has produced a lot of Christians who are only out to seek instant miracles for everything. Instead of working they go about looking for financial breakthroughs and all sorts of breakthroughs. But that is about to change for the better.

A new breed of Christians is coming out of this mind shift. A new breed of believers will be born, who will no longer be lazy and idle but pro-active and productive. A new breed of God's children who truly understand and know that prayer, faith, and hard work are inseparable is here to stay and dominate the world.

A new breed of youths, young and old, boys and girls, men and women who know when to pray, when not to pray and when to stop praying is around to deliver various sectors of our economy. A people who know that prayer without work is dead is here to shake their world for God. Don't be left out of this army of believers.

NUGGETS

1. There is no way you tell me you want to pray without faith. And there is certainly no way that prayer can be effective without you working it out.

2. Prayer without work is dead. And action without prayer is foolish.

3. Prayer is not merely a habit but a way of life.

4. In prayer, you learn who God is and what He wants you to do.

5. When you are not dead to yourself, you fear the consequences of failure.

6. If you have a calling from the lord and do nothing to fulfill it, you are on the verge of being ruined.

7. If you are faithful with little, you will graduate to much.

8. You were made for greatness and big things.

Chapter 11
AFTER PRAYING WHAT NEXT?

If only in all our religious endeavors, we caught a glimpse of the mind of God our country will not be where it is today. Misunderstanding of the subject of faith has made most Christians act very stupidly at times. It has also taken our common sense from us.

"Prayer is man's greatest power!"
W. Clement Stone

The unbelievers who don't pray deprive themselves of divine help and intervention but they still produce more results than most of us because they work it out. How much more when you go out there to work hard on that thing you are believing God for?

Jesus knew when to pray and when not to pray. Oftentimes, it is recorded that He walked away from His disciples to a secluded place to pray. But at other times He would go about doing the work of Him that sent Him. So, He knew when to stop praying and go to work.

Each time it is recorded of how Jesus went to a secluded place to pray, it is also recorded when He stopped praying, leaves the place of prayer and go to work with His disciples. You also must know when to stop praying and go to work to produce evidence of your faith.

As a result, Jesus worked more effectively and produced more results. The bible always took the time to emphasize to us that Jesus descended from the mountain of prayer. So, prayer, as most Christians know it to be today, was not something Jesus was engaged in without ceasing. He knew when to stop and when to go to work. We need to learn from this example.

This attitude of Jesus debunks the myth that is represented by some categories of Christians who would rather just pray and not go to work at all. Jesus knows the difference between when to begin to pray and when to stop praying. All Christians must know this same difference in order to excel in life.

If we don't know when to pray, when to stop praying and when not to pray at all, we can never be light and salt on the earth.

After all the prayers my dear brothers and sisters, you must learn to roll up your sleeves and get the job done. No matter how much you pray food will not appear on your table automatically neither will the table set itself. Companies and industries will not be built in a country supernaturally, even if the country is full of prayer warriors and righteous men and women, someone needs to build those companies and institutions.

Somebody will have to build those hospitals. Another person will have to work there. Somebody will have to construct those roads. Somebody will need to set those companies up. Somebody will need to go and put things in place in the energy and electricity sector for things to work in order.

The lesson here is very clear. After the prayers, you need to go and bring to pass what you have prayed about.

And if you really have faith, you will go and make it happen.

When somebody prays, the purpose of that prayer is for him to get the grace, energy, direction, and insight into what to do after he has descended from the mountain of prayer. So, you have more clarity and that is what prayer does for you.

EVILS OF INSTANT GRATIFICATION

The problem is most believers stop at praying only. A lot of Christians today, only pray without ever taking action. They never leave the prayer room to carry out the plans God has revealed to them. And this attitude has given birth to the syndrome of instant gratification.

We all want it now and here. Let me get the miracle money now. I need the miracle job now, even though I don't have the skills required. Therefore, we've decided to use prayer as a tool for instant gratification.

We only go to God to come and fix this or fix that. We want God to fix our hospitals today and if possible also come and treat all the sick patients there. And we want our roads and industries fixed right now and immediately as well. We've become a group of believers who want everything by miracle. Then, why did God give us a brain? Why do we have a sound mind?

Our messages of instant gratification have created a generation of people who only want to see instant results, immediate relief, and a painless effort. We want to get rich without having to work and we also want to invent new ground breaking technologies but we don't want to use our brains to think. Prosperity and breakthroughs will never emanate from idleness and laziness.

After we've prayed for our power and electricity sector, it's time to begin to call together our engineers and specialist in our churches and come up with ways that sector can perform better nationally. When we've prayed for the leadership in the country, it's time we begin to train up young leaders just sitting still in our churches to be actively involved and take up leadership positions in the country.

When we've committed the educational sector into God's hands, it's time to stop praying and start gathering the best of the best together to brain storm, use their minds and come up with better curriculum, then suggest such recommendations to be effected in our schools. You and I need to stop praying and start taking prayer-inspired actions.

If you've been following me so far, I believe you already know when to pray, when not to pray or when to stop praying. Therefore, start taking prayer-inspired actions right now. Don't wait till tomorrow. Start today.

In the sphere of influence where God has placed you, He expects you to be responsible. He expects you to swing into action and bring about his plans there rather than kneeling with your hands in between your thighs and believing that praying more will build our roads or improve our health sector. It's time to take prayer inspired actions.

RIGHT NOW, WHAT NEXT?

Instant gratification is the desire to experience pleasure or fulfillment without delay or deferment. Basically, it's when you want it; and you want it now. It is an innate desire to have what we want when we want it, which is usually without any delay. It is also a habit where you forgo short-term pain that will eventually lead to long-term pleasure.

People caught up within the instant gratification trap often expect to gain something from nothing. Unfortunately, the world doesn't work that way.

On the other hand, getting into the habit of delaying gratification gives you more sense of control over your life, decisions, and actions. Furthermore, it helps you value hard work and effort. You understand even though things might be difficult in the present moment that it's necessary you get through this pain in order to experience the long-term pleasure you would ultimately like to have in your life.

The act of delaying gratification helps to strengthen your mind and shape your character. It builds your willpower, promotes higher levels of self-discipline, and teaches you about the value of patience. It is, in fact, the ultimate habit that determines how successful you will become and how much you will ultimately achieve in the future.

So right now, it's important that you consciously work through these steps that will set you on the right track and move in the right direction after you've prayed.

STEP 1: CLEARLY DEFINE WHAT YOU WANT

After praying, you must first understand where you are going and what you want to achieve. If you don't understand where you are going or what you are going to be working towards, then it's easy to get distracted by the temptations that life throws your way. Drawing up a plan to attain your goals and vision can help you to remain focused and disciplined along this journey.

Begin by clarifying your vision and mission. Ask yourself:

What do I want to achieve?

How will I achieve this?

Why do I want this? What are the benefits?

Why is it important to work towards this vision?

It's important that you also specify your short-term objectives and priorities. This is critical because often instant gratification will crop up into your life when you are indecisive or uncertain about your direction. During these moments any temptation seems much more pleasurable than trying to work through the pain of figuring out what to do. This is especially true when you are confronted with unexpected problems.

Maybe, you are personally concerned about the political sphere of things in your country. Maybe you sense that God is calling you to go into politics to represent Him and bring about change and development there. Now is the time to set to work. Now is the time to get off your high horse and begin to do something about it.

Start by asking yourself, what do I want to achieve? How will I achieve this? Why do I want this? What are the benefits? Why is it important to work towards this vision?

You may not exactly be called to run for political offices but to influence other aspects of the political world. Nevertheless, you still have to clearly define what you want to achieve. You might be the one to implement an electoral system that will be truly free and fair across your country. It might be your idea that will re-educate the populace on the importance of voting.

Perhaps, you are the one to develop a program for young people that will teach them how not to allow themselves to be used as political bulldogs by all these power hungry politicians in our country. There are indeed several things we could possibly do to improve the way things are down in our political sphere of life and God is counting on you to make some of those changes.

STEP 2: IDENTIFY POTENTIAL OBSTACLES

Along your journey towards fulfilling your God given vision and agenda in any sphere of life, you will confront many problems. But relax; those problems are there to propel you to greater heights. They are there to promote you. Problems are not bad. They are your shortcuts to prominence.

Wherever there is a problem or obstacle, there is a blessing. Wherever there is a problem, there is a future. Wherever there is a problem, there are opportunities. Wherever there is a problem, there is honor. Wherever there is a problem, there is money. And wherever there is a problem, there is a job.

So, don't run away from obstacles or problems that might come your way. Instead, face them head on and you will be shocked that you've been wired to solve those problems. Identify the problems and come up with the best and most efficient solutions and you will be amazed that those problems are there to promote you.

"Nothing stops the man who desires to achieve. Every obstacle is simply a course to develop his achievement muscle. It's a strengthening of his powers of accomplishment." Thomas Carlyle

Some of these problems will be unexpected, and if you are not ready and able to deal with them, it then becomes easy to lose focus of the ultimate goal - essentially distracting you from achieving what you stated earlier in step one above.

Problems can be quite unpredictable, and you won't always know what problems you might face in advance. And yet problems are something you can effectively work through at the time as long as you don't get caught up indulging in temptations that are likely to distract your mind from the most important tasks at hand.

For this very reason, it's critical that you identify the temptations you might confront along your journey that could sidetrack you when the road becomes difficult. Ask yourself:

What problems could sidetrack me?

And how will I handle these obstacles or problems?

At this stage, don't make the mistake of trying to find solutions to your problems. Your problems are irrelevant. You will most certainly overcome them, as long as you don't get caught off-guard by the temptations that life will throw your way.

In the end, it's not the problem you must worry about, but rather concern yourself with the things that could distract you from solving your problem. Every problem is a blessing in disguise.

STEP 3: BUILD A STRONG SUPPORT NETWORK

In order to avoid falling into the instant gratification trap, it's paramount that you build a strong support network of people who will help support you during difficult moments along your journey. Ask yourself:

Who could support me along this journey?

How could they support me?
What would their role be?

> *"Life is not a solo act. It's a huge collaboration, and we all need to assemble around us the people who care about us and support us in times of strife."*
> *Tim Gunn*

You will unlikely achieve the success you envision without a strong support network. These are the people that can help you to get past your problems. They are also there to help you stay focused and keep your eyes on the prize (end goal) without being sidetracked or distracted by temporary pleasures that life will no doubt tempt you with.

It's also important here that you clarify what kinds of resources you might need on your journey. Ask yourself:

What resources will be needed to accomplish this task?

Also, ask yourself, how will I acquire these resources?

Those resources might include tools; skills, knowledge, and a plethora of other things that you will need to achieve your desired goal. Maybe you'll even need resources that will help you to ward off short-term pleasures and temptations that might suddenly creep up on you during difficult moments. Really have a good long hard think about what you might need along your journey to help guarantee you remain focused on what's most important at all times.

STEP 4: SET CLEAR BOUNDARIES

It's important at this stage to set clear boundaries or rules about what you will do and what you will avoid doing at all costs.

Without clear boundaries, it's easy to fall prey to distractions. However, with clear rules in place about what you're allowed and not allowed to do, will help you to feel more in control of the events and circumstances in your life.

You might want to ask yourself:

What am I allowed to do?

What's absolutely off limits?

Determine what kind of behaviors you will no longer indulge in and think about the long-term rewards and benefits you will derive from avoiding these potential temptations.

STEP 5: FOCUS ON THE BIG PICTURE

"Think big and don't listen to people who tell you it can't be done. Life's too short to think small."
Tim Ferriss

Since you've clearly defined what you want to achieve, you've also set clear boundaries, identify possible obstacles and how to relate with problems, it's now time to create the motivation you need to help you focus and move towards the ultimate goal every day.

One of the best ways to maintain long-term motivation is to display visual reminders of your goals and priorities on your wall or desktop. It could be in the form of a vision board, or some kind of collage that represents your goals. Or it could just be photos of what you would like to achieve in the future.

These reminders come in handy whenever you are tempted to go off track and possibly indulge in something you shouldn't be doing. During these moments take time to reflect upon the visual reminders of your goals. This could, in fact, be all you need to help you stay focused and on track.

Reminding yourself about what it is you are working towards in the long-term will help you to remember what's most important moving forward. This will likewise allow you to re-prioritize your actions accordingly to help create the momentum you need to achieve your goals.

Yes, of course, the current task you are working on might seem somewhat tedious and boring. However, it's a part of the bigger picture and will, therefore, lead to some significant gains in the future.

Focus on the opportunities that will be available to our youths when the economy is vibrant. Focus on the peace and stability that will flood the nation when the elections are free and fair. And think of the high standard of health care treatment that will be available to pensioners and homeless old people in the society.

Talking about the entertainment industry, check out history and see what role Hollywood played in the great depression years in America. See how they cleverly used Hollywood to reeducate and inspire the entire country right in the middle of their trials.

Whereas many were losing their jobs and many were jobless, the people still found their way to the theatres in mass during those days. But why was this so? It was because the movie industry performed a valuable psychological and ideological role, providing reassurance and hope to a demoralized nation!

Even at the Depression's most dire moments, 60 to 80 million Americans attended the movies each week, and in the face of doubt and despair, films helped sustain national morale.

We must begin to focus on this big picture also in our movie industries, especially in Nigeria. Nollywood must begin to become more educational than just a baseless show of rituals everywhere. This is the 21st century for crying out loud. We should be able to offer much more.

I am looking forward to producers that will emerge with movies of possibilities for the Nigerian populace. I am looking forward to movies that people will finish watching and get up to take the bull by the horn and bring about deliverance and salvation in their sphere of contact and influence. I am looking forward to movies that will inspire scientific discoveries and inventions.

What stops us from producing movies that a school dropout will finish watching and decide to go back to school? What stops us from producing movies that our kids will watch and be inspired to study even harder? Who says we can't produce movies that armed robbers and prostitutes will watch and have a total change of mind? It's all about coming up with the right concepts. And I am convinced that someone reading this book right now, will arise to the challenge and do this for our beloved nation.

The time has come for our musicians and other people in the entertainment industry to rise up to the occasion that the nation has found itself. It is time for worthy role models to emerge in our entertainment industry. I may not be a musician but someone reading this right now is.

My challenge to you, therefore, is to begin to think how you can do something about the industry to move her forward. Focus on the big picture and begin to strategize about how the entertainment industry can become a major contributor to the development and health of the land.

After praying, follow each of these five steps. In the sphere of influence where God has placed you, He expects you to be responsible. He expects you to swing into action and bring about his plans in the banking and finance sector, tourism, education, art and culture, entertainment, politics, media, family values, sports, and industry. Can He count on you?

NUGGETS

1. The unbelievers who don't pray deprive themselves of divine help and intervention but they still produce more results than most of us because they work it out.

2. Each time it is recorded of how Jesus went to a secluded place to pray, it is also recorded when He stopped praying, leaves the place of prayer and go to work with His disciples.

3. If we don't know when to pray, when to stop praying and when not to pray at all, we can never be light and salt on the earth.

4. The lesson here is very clear. After the prayers, you need to go and bring to pass what you have prayed about. And if you really have faith, you will go and make it happen.

5. Instant gratification is the desire to experience pleasure or fulfillment without delay or deferment.

6. The habit of delaying gratification gives you more sense of control over your life, decisions, and actions. Furthermore, it helps you value hard work and effort.

Chapter 12
CAN HE COUNT ON YOU?

Unfortunately, the emphasis on mission through evangelism and church growth has sometimes resulted in Pentecostals neglecting the social and political dimensions of mission and failing to address the social ills of society.

Right now, God is counting on you to discard this church-building mentality and get involved in the restorative processes for National Transformation by assuming positions of responsibility in every sector of society.

We must also discard messages bordering on instant gratification in the name of instant miracles. This is not the good news to the poor and afflicted. Let's teach them to be independent by getting their hands to work and depend on God alone. The messages we preach has made a lot of our members idolize their pastors because they are seeking miracles.

And while they are going about seeking miracles, people like Dangote are creating more jobs. Then we leave the same church and go out to the secular world seeking jobs from unbelievers. Is that the good news Jesus came to die for?

With a plan to create 750,000 jobs in the next five years and thereafter raise it to one million, Dangote Group will overtake the federal government as the biggest employer of labor in Nigeria. The conglomerate owned by Alhaji Aliko Dangote has a current workforce of 26,000 spread across its subsidiaries in cement, salt and sugar manufacturing and packaging plants.

President of Dangote Group has also assured Nigerians that topmost on his priority is how to contribute his own quota towards reducing the high rate of unemployment in the country. In one of his Cement Plant in Edo State, that alone employs a minimum of 45,000 Nigerians in both direct and indirect capacity. He said the number of Nigerians that will be employed in its ongoing fertilizer and petrochemical plants will be far more than the cement plants figure.

Apple Company started by Steve Jobs and Steve Wozniak also boasted of creating or supporting more than 500,000 jobs for U.S. workers: from the engineer who helped invent the iPad to the delivery person who brings it to your door. Let's not even go to other companies like Alibaba, Facebook, Google or Microsoft.

So, how did Apple get to more than half a million workers? According to a report on Forbes.com, its numbers include 304,000 current U.S. jobs - 47,000 Apple employees in the U.S. (out of a total 70,000 employees around the world) and 257,000 jobs at "other companies" that touch and support its products.

Apple defines those as workers who help develop and manufacture components, materials, and equipment used in the creation of its top-selling products, including the iPhone and iPad tablet; professional, scientific and technical services; consumer sales; business sales; transportation and healthcare.

As Apple put it, its indirect workers include those "in Texas who manufacture processors for iOS products, Corning employees in Kentucky and New York who create the majority of the glass for the iPhone, and FedEx and UPS employees."

It also counted 210,000 jobs created around the "app economy" spurred on by the iOS operating system used in its smartphone and tablet. Apple culled the app number from the TechNet study, which found there are now about 466,000 jobs in the "App Economy" in the U.S, up from zero in 2007.

With all these numbers, facts and figures, if you will be sincere with yourself, who is actually carrying out the great commission? Is it the person that sleeps in church all night or the man that starts a technological revolution and giving millions around the world a source of livelihood? Is it the man that creates more jobs or the man that has been praying for job creation since 2007? Please, I need an answer! Don't be quiet on me now!

Is it the man in China that develops the next medical equipment that will diagnose cancer early and save more lives or the man that leads the choir? Maybe the man who develops the airplane that flies pastors around the world to evangelize is not contributing anything to the propagation of the gospel? Hmmmm...I guess you know better.

THIS IS THE EVIDENCE
OF MY FAITH

Trust me on this, if you really believe in the job creation you've been praying about, then, you cannot sit still doing nothing about it. If you really believe it, you will not be indolent, lazy or indifferent. Faith will push you. Faith will make you unstoppable. Faith puts fire in your bones.

Steve Jobs was adopted. He is a school dropout. Jack Ma of Alibaba applied to Harvard and was rejected multiples times. He searched for employment and was turned down on multiple occasions. Thomas Edison couldn't get the perfect model for the electric bulb until its 1,000 attempt.

Thomas Edison is a true definition of what it means to fail woefully, yet he is still regarded as the greatest inventor so far with about a thousand patents to his name. Helen Keller did not live a life of mediocrity because she was blind, deaf and couldn't speak at an early age. What is your excuse, my dear friend? What are you doing with your time? What is stopping you from putting your faith to work?

Do you also know that Albert Einstein, the most influential physicist of the 20th century and Nobel Laureate didn't speak until he was four years old?

Einstein didn't have the best childhood. In fact, many people thought he was just a dud. He never spoke for the first three years of his life, and throughout elementary school, many of his teachers thought he was lazy and wouldn't make anything of himself.

But faith makes you unperturbed by circumstances, hindrances, challenges or by the enemies. With faith, you don't have to worry and you will become so confident that you keep on going, you keep on fighting, and you keep on pressing until the substance is produced. And you won't be able to stop until you are able to show the world, this is the substance of what I was telling you about. This is the evidence of my faith.

Christians as believers are supposed to be the most active. If you call yourself a Christian, you are supposed to be the hardest worker out there. A believer is meant to believe in the end result that he wants to produce. He so much believes and goes to work until he sees that end result.

Believers are supposed to be some of the most diligent and hardworking individuals out there. They are supposed to be some of the most ambitious, zealous and unstoppable workers out there. This is because faith goes after evidence. And if you have faith, you will be a man of substance, you will create and you will produce that substance to prove your faith.

So if you believe you want God to create jobs, go out there and create jobs. Start up a company that will employ others. If you are praying for any part of the society, first find out the problem, then, go and do your due diligence, do extensive research, exhaust the literature on such matters and come back with the most efficient solution. You are the answer to the cries of many. Don't deny your world the solutions inside you.

Christians and believers are supposed to be the most pro-active people in every sphere of life. If you believe that the kingdom of God will come, you will be the most active out there in the field fighting for that kingdom to come. You will be giving your all, working day and night. That is the evidence of your faith.

The solutions you provide to the problems around you is the evidence of your faith. It becomes the result of your prayers as well.

If we are actually a people of faith and prayers the way we profess it, we ought to have much more substance than all other people to confirm our faith. The substance that you have is the confirmation of your faith. If you don't have any substance, what faith are you talking about then?

If you don't have any substance, the world is going to push you aside. They will walk on you. If you don't have any substance and you call yourself a man of faith, then you are making a mockery of yourself. And you are a disgrace to God.

If you say you are a believer but you don't have any substance to show for it, I think you need to begin to reconsider what god you are praying to? Which god are you praying to that you've not been able to produce any evidence? What kind of god do you believe in that you don't have any substance to back it up?

It is your laziness that is to blame. If you actually have faith, you ought to have more substance than all other people in the world put together, because our substance confirms our faith.

FAITH IS NOT SOME SENSELESS DREAMS OR IMAGINATIONS

Let me quickly take you back to that scripture in Hebrews 11.

"Now faith is the substance of things hoped for, the evidence of things not seen."

Hebrews 11:1 (KJV)

If we are to go by this scripture, you will agree with me that if you cannot produce a substance, it equally means you have no faith. That's just the basic truth. If you can't present any substance, I'm sorry, there is no debate about it.

The substance is the proof. The substance is the evidence. The substance is something that you can see. It's something that can be touched and tangible enough to be felt. People of faith produce a substance to back up their faith.

We, believers, are supposed to have more start-up companies and scientific breakthroughs to our names because we profess our faith in God. We are supposed to have more industries and impact than any other group of people in the world.

Our nation should be littered with more industries and more evidence to show for our faith than any other group of people on earth, not just the unbelievers. But, what do we see in our churches today?

What is obtainable in our country today? Where is the substance? Where is the evidence? Ours is a nation littered with churches on every street and packed full with people just hoping tomorrow will better than today just because they pray.

But is that the kind of life Jesus came to die for? Where we, as believers will always be hoping things will get better tomorrow? What about today? The book of Hebrews 11 says, 'NOW, faith....' It's talking about 'NOW.'

Where is your evidence, my dear brother? You've been praying for years my dear sister, what is the result? What are you doing to get what you believed God for? Are you just hoping and believing without doing anything to get the necessary result?

> *"Faith does not suspend our sense of good judgment, it reinforces it." Benson Idahosa*

You need to work out your faith. The fact that you are working it out is your prove. Faith is not some sense-less dreams or imaginations. Faith is not a dream. There must be a substance to stand as evidence. Where are the substances that are backing up what you are saying you hope for?

Dear pastor, your church members are supposed to be men and women of substance, prove and results.

THE EVIDENCE OF THINGS NOT SEEN

The second part of the same Hebrews 11:1 says,

"...the evidence of things not seen"

According to this second part, it also means faith will make things that were not seen before to become visible. So, will I be wrong to say Steve Jobs and someone like Bill Gates were seeing things that the world have not seen or witnessed before them? Will you agree with me that they had evidence of things not seen?

Everything that is still not visible to the world right now, the church is supposed to be bringing them to existence. Why? This is because we are men and women of faith. Faith brings things that have never been seen before into the world. Faith brings the evidence of things that have never been seen before.

If we say we are believers, then, we are supposed to have something tangible in our hand that confirms that faith - the algorithms, formulas, sketches, projects etc.

We are supposed to have a lot of evidence saying these things will happen tomorrow. Planes will fly tomorrow. Cars will run on solar energy tomorrow. There will be another set of smart phones in the next ten years. We are supposed to be a people full of evidence. But we are not being taught these things in our churches.

Believers are not being taught to produce. We are not being taught to be inventors and innovators. We are not taught to be creators. We are not taught to be leaders and take the lead wherever we find ourselves. We are totally the direct opposite of what faith is supposed to do for us.

Faith is supposed to make us the top producers of things that have not been seen before. Faith is supposed to make us the producers of substances that the whole world is hoping for.

The whole world is hoping for the cure of cancer right now. As believers, we are the ones that are supposed to say this is the evidence that I will produce the cure. The world is waiting for the cure for AIDS. You are supposed to produce that evidence. But where is your laboratory? Where is your library? Where is the evidence that you will produce the result? What are you doing presently that will produce that result?

The world should always look to the church for the next inventions. The whole world should be waiting on the people of God to produce the next scientific discoveries. That is the faith that will make you work harder than anybody else. That is the faith that will make you do the impossible.

The church of God is meant to produce giants and sons who are able to produce results. But when we just sit down in the churches, of course, unbelievers will do it. God will even raise up stones in our stead because we don't want to go and work. We just want to hide under the cover of prayers and say we are singing, and jumping instead of us to go out there and produce real results.

GO AND MAKE IT HAPPEN

"To accomplish great things, we must not only act, but also dream; not only plan but also believe."
Anatole France

You have the creative ability in you. So, go and make use of it. The reason why we don't have any evidence is because we don't work hard enough. You think by prayers alone, all your problems will be solved?

While you are praying and sleeping in churches and on Prayer Mountains, other people are working hard, so we shouldn't be surprised if they have results and we have nothing to show.

Once again, when you've prayed, it's time to leave the place of prayer and get the work done. If you are not producing anything, the world will just be laughing at you. The world will just be mocking you. That's why the bible tells us that faith without works is dead.

You as a believer are meant to work harder than others in proving the evidence of your faith and not to hide in the place of prayer or in prayer houses. We shouldn't just leave everything to God and objurgate our responsibilities.

God has already done everything on His part. He has already put everything in creation. So, stop using prayer as a cover up. He has already put all the resources you will ever need on earth. You need to go and make it happen.

Prayer, on the other hand, should give you more energy, more faith, and more grace to be able to do more than others who do not pray. We should not use it as a cover up and expect God to do for us what we are supposed to do for ourselves. Get up from your seats and get your hands dirty through work. Get off from the pews and produce evidence of that faith you profess.

All I have been saying from chapter one of this book is to let you know that a conscious believer who also believes in prayer must also know the difference between the time to pray and when not to pray. A true believer should work and pray. Work as though you never prayed, and pray as though you did not work.

"Pray as though everything depended on God. Work as though everything depended on you."
Saint Augustine

Pray, and believe God but after that, you need to go and work hard. Go and persevere, go and labor if you need to, but you must produce the result. You must produce the evidence. You must produce the substance of what you believe God for. Your heavenly father has confidence in you that you will go and make things happen in your world.

Blessings!

NUGGETS

1. Right now, God is counting on you to discard this church-building mentality and get involved in the restorative processes for National Transformation by assuming positions of responsibility in every sector of society.

2. If you call yourself a Christian, you are supposed to be the hardest worker out there.

3. If you don't have any substance, the world is going to push you aside. They will walk on you.

4. It is your laziness that is to blame. If you actually have faith, you ought to have more substance than all other people in the world put together, because our substance confirms our faith.

5. If we are to go by this scripture, you will agree with me that if you cannot produce a substance, it equally means you have no faith.

CONCLUSION

Sometime ago someone asked me, "If God does as he pleases, then why do we pray?"

God definitely answers prayers when we pray to Him, but praying to God is mostly for our benefit. Prayer is not necessarily a time to blurt out all or request and rant about how we want to be elevated in life.

It's more of an intense communication with God, that connection that we feel when we are in His presence… where we feel safe and just express how much we love Him and how much more we want to know Him…an avenue to draw strength, courage and just feel refreshed. It's a time for us to allow God examine our hearts and see if there's any way we can be found wanting. That's the essence of prayers.

There's this inexplicable feeling that comes with being still and praying and just being in God's presence. God is still God even when we do not pray to Him. Our prayers or absence of it does not take away His sovereignty. It pleases God to give us good things and to perfect all that concerns us and that is why He does it.

Think about it; if God really waited for us to pray for everything in the morning before we stepped out, we would not even be alive probably, because sometimes we forget to ask God for His guidance and protection.

One of the most beautiful things about God is the fact that He knows us more than we know ourselves. He knows even what we need before we ask for it. Even the things we don't ask for, He does and gives. Even the things we don't think we need, He gives us because He knows we need them. Even without praying for it. He blesses us all unexpectedly, and without deserving it.

However, praying to Him strengthens our faith in Him especially when He answers prayers and we get to see His hand in everything in our lives. God is amazing indeed. But God will never take responsibility for what you are meant to do in order to advance His kingdom on earth. That is your responsibility. You have a role to play as well.

Stop escaping into prayer! Stop using prayer as a cover up. Be a prayer warrior but not a prayer hermit. There is a problem in the land and we can't sit still any longer. You and I must arise and go to work until what we see in prayers begin to manifest in the physical.

Prayer is an opportunity to see what God is doing in Heaven and his plans for earth. When you have access to this opportunity it provides you with the blueprint of what you are supposed to do base on God's plan. This is what Jesus meant when he said,

"Thy kingdom come, Thy will be done in earth, as it is in heaven."

Matt. 6:10 (KJV)

With this, we become a conduit of God's will and kingdom on earth.

My dear brothers and sisters, we must enforce the kingdom of God on earth. He won't come down and build our roads for us. No matter how much time we spend in prayers, that won't make Him invent a plane and fly it as well or build our schools and teach there also.

So, the next time you pray, connect with your heavenly father, commune with Him, then, go out to carry out His plans and agenda for the kingdom. God is counting on you to do your part.

Thank you for reading this far. I really can't wait to hear what becomes of you through the application of the wisdom nuggets contained in this book. Feel free to write me anytime, I read every single mail and will be glad to reply you.

pastor @godembassy.org

You can also avail yourself of other training materials of mine on my blog: www.SundayAdelajaBlog.com

FOR THE LOVE OF GOD, CHURCH, AND NATION

SUNDAY ADELAJA'S
BIOGRAPHY

Pastor Sunday Adelaja is the Founder and Senior Pastor of The Embassy of the Blessed Kingdom of God for All Nations Church in Kyiv, Ukraine.

Sunday Adelaja is a Nigerian-born Leader, Thinker, Philosopher, Transformation Strategist, Pastor, Author and Innovator who lives in Kiev, Ukraine.

At 19, he won a scholarship to study in the former Soviet Union. He completed his master's program in Belorussia State University with distinction in journalism.

At 33, he had built the largest evangelical church in Europe — The Embassy of the Blessed Kingdom of God for All Nations.

Sunday Adelaja is one of the few individuals in our world who has been privileged to speak in the United Nations, Israeli Parliament, Japanese Parliament and the United States Senate.

The movement he pioneered has been instrumental in reshaping lives of people in the Ukraine, Russia and about 50 other nations where he has his branches.

His congregation, which consists of ninety-nine percent white Europeans, is a cross-cultural model of the church for the 21st century.

His life mission is to advance the Kingdom of God on earth by

raising a generation of history makers who will live for a cause larger, bigger and greater than themselves. Those who will live like Jesus and transform every sphere of the society in every nation as a model of the Kingdom of God on earth.

His economic empowerment program has succeeded in raising over 200 millionaires in the short period of three years.

Sunday Adelaja is the author of over 300 books, many of which are translated into several languages including Russian, English, French, Chinese, German, etc.

His work has been widely reported by world media outlets such as The Washington Post, The Wall Street Journal, New York Times, Forbes, Associated Press, Reuters, CNN, BBC, German, Dutch and French national television stations.

Pastor Sunday is happily married to his "Princess" Bose Dere-Adelaja. They are blessed with three children: Perez, Zoe and Pearl.

DR. SUNDAY ADELAJA

Bill Clinton —
42Nd President Of The
United States (1993–2001),
Former Arcansas State
Governor

Ariel "Arik" Sharon —
Israeli Politician, Israeli
Prime Minister (2001–2006)

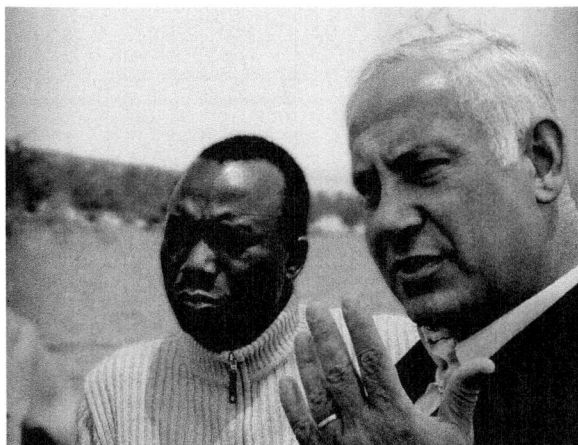

Benjamin Netanyahu —
Statesman Of Israel. Israeli
Prime Minister (1996–1999),
Acting Prime Minister
(From 2009)

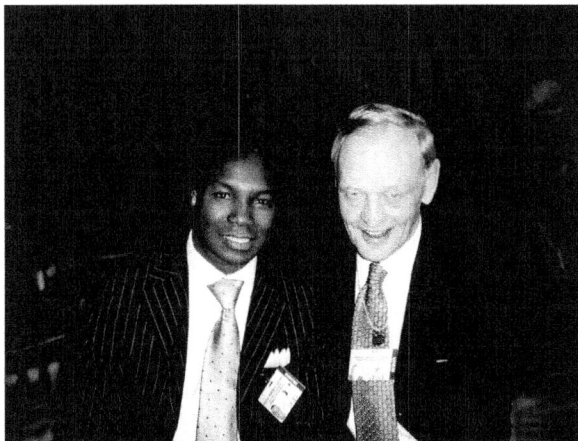

Jean ChrEtien —
Canadian Politician,
20Th Prime Minister Of
Canada, Minister Of Justice
Of Canada, Head Of Liberan
Party Of Canada

Rudolph Giuliani —
American Political Actor,
Mayor Of New York Served
From 1994 To 2001. Actor
Of Republican Party

Colin Powell —
Is An American Statesman
And A Retired Four-Star
General In The Us Army,
65Th United States Secretary
Of State

Peter J. Daniels —
Is A Well-Known And
Respected Australian
Christian International
Business Statesman Of
Substance

Madeleine
Korbel Albright —
An American Politician And
Diplomat, 64[Th] United States
Secretary Of State

Kenneth Robert
Livingstone —
An English Politician,
1[St] Mayor Of London
(4 May 2000 – 4 May
2008), Labour Party
Representative

Sir Richard Charles Nicholas Branson —
English Business Magnate, Investor And Philanthropist. He Founded The *Virgin Group*, Which Controls More Than 400 Companies

Mel Gibson —
American Actor And Filmmaker

Chuck Norris —
American Martial Artist, Actor, Film Producer And Screenwriter

Christopher Tucker — American Actor And Comedian

Bernice Albertine King — American Minister Best Known As The Youngest Child Of Civil Rights Leaders Martin Luther King Jr. And Coretta Scott King Andrew

Andrew Young — American Politician, Diplomat, And Activist, 14[Th] United States Ambassador To The United Nations, 55[Th] Mayor Of Atlanta

General Wesley Kanne Clark — 4-Star General And Nato Supreme Allied Commander

Dr. Sunday Adelaja's family: Perez, Pearl, Zoe and Pastor Bose Adelaja

FOLLOW
SUNDAY ADELAJA
ON SOCIAL MEDIA

Subscribe And Read Pastor Sunday's Blog:

www.sundayadelajablog.com

Follow these links and listen to over 200
of Pastor Sunday`s Messages free of charge:

http://sundayadelajablog.com/content/

Follow Pastor Sunday on Twitter:

www.twitter.com/official_pastor

Join Pastor Sunday's Facebook page to stay in touch:

www.facebook.com/pastor.
sunday.adelaja

Visit our websites for more
information about Pastor
Sunday's ministry:

http://www.godembassy.com

http://www.pastorsunday.com

http://sundayadelaja.de

CONTACT

FOR DISTRIBUTION OR TO ORDER
BULK COPIES OF THIS BOOK,
PLEASE CONTACT US:

USA
CORNERSTONE PUBLISHING
info@thecornerstonepublishers.com
+1 (516) 547-4999
www.thecornerstonepublishers.com

AFRICA
SUNDAY ADELAJA MEDIA LTD
btawolana@hotmail.com
+2348187518530, +2348097721451, +2348034093699

CHIOMA NWIGWE (NIGERIA)
dsabooksplanet@gmail.com
+2347065228537, +2348122219291

LONDON, UK
ADEKUNLE BANJOKO
banjokoadekunle@gmail.com
+447411937793

KIEV, UKRAINE
pa@godembassy.org
Mobile: +380674401958

BEST SELLING BOOKS BY DR. SUNDAY ADELAJA
AVAILABLE ON AMAZON.COM AND OKADABOOKS.COM

Best Selling Books by Dr. Sunday Adelaja
Available on Amazon.com and Okadabooks.com

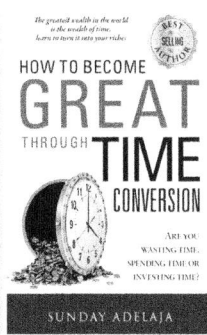

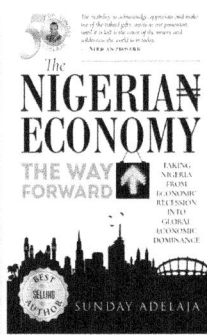

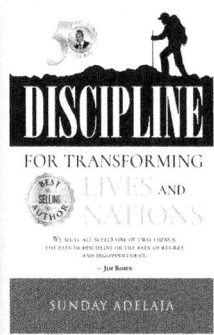

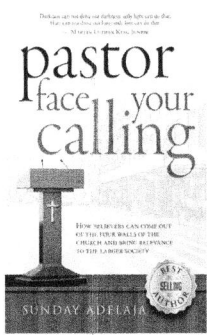

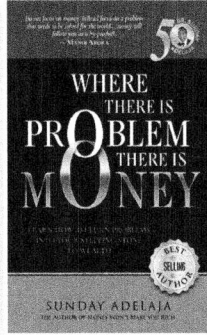

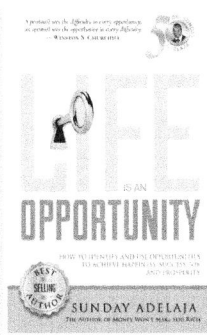

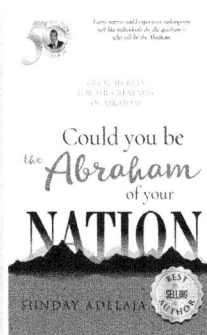

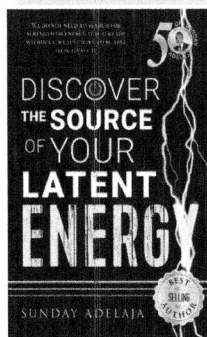

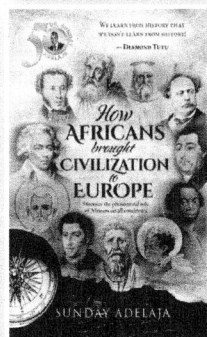

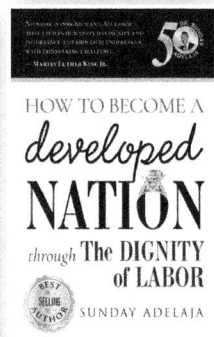

Work like a slave today and live like a king tomorrow

WHY YOU MUST URGENTLY BECOME A WORKAHOLIC

Through work we become co-workers with God

SUNDAY ADELAJA

The greatest wealth in the world is the wealth of time, learn to turn it into your riches.

HOW TO BECOME **GREAT** THROUGH **TIME CONVERSION**

Are you wasting time, spending time or investing time?

SUNDAY ADELAJA

The inability to acknowledge, appreciate and make use of the talked gifts stored in our personalit until it is laid is the cause of the misery and addiction the world is in today.

The **NIGERIAN ECONOMY** THE WAY FORWARD

TAKING NIGERIA FROM ECONOMIC RECESSION INTO GLOBAL ECONOMIC DOMINANCE

SUNDAY ADELAJA

DISCIPLINE FOR TRANSFORMING LIVES AND NATIONS

WE MUST ALL SUFFER ONE OF TWO THINGS: THE PAIN OF DISCIPLINE OR THE PAIN OF REGRET AND DISAPPOINTMENT.
— JIM ROHN

SUNDAY ADELAJA

---

pastor face your calling

HOW BELIEVERS CAN COME OUT OF THE FOUR WALLS OF THE CHURCH AND BRING RELEVANCE TO THE LABOR SOCIETY

SUNDAY ADELAJA

WHERE THERE IS PROBLEM THERE IS MONEY

SUNDAY ADELAJA
THE AUTHOR OF MONEY WON'T MAKE YOU RICH

A pessimist sees the difficulty in every opportunity; an optimist sees the opportunity in every difficulty.
— WINSTON S. CHURCHILL

LIFE IS AN OPPORTUNITY

HOW TO IDENTIFY AND USE OPPORTUNITIES TO ACHIEVE HAPPINESS, SUCCESS, SIGNIFICANCE AND FULFILMENT

SUNDAY ADELAJA
THE AUTHOR OF MONEY WON'T MAKE YOU RICH

The **CREATIVE** and **INNOVATIVE POWER** of a **GENIUS**

SUNDAY ADELAJA

---

7 tips to **SELF-FULFILLMENT** in life

SUNDAY ADELAJA

A VISIONLESS LIFE IS A MEANINGLESS LIFE

SUNDAY ADELAJA

Could you be the **Abraham** of your **NATION**

SUNDAY ADELAJA

---

excellence your key to **ELEVATION**

SUNDAY ADELAJA

DISCOVER THE SOURCE OF YOUR LATENT ENERGY

SUNDAY ADELAJA

If you are not solving problems, then you are a problem

HELLO! I am searching for PROBLEMS

USE PROBLEMS AS SPRINGBOARD FOR YOUR ELEVATION

SUNDAY ADELAJA

WE LEARN FROM HISTORY THAT WE DON'T LEARN FROM HISTORY.
— DESMOND TUTU

How AFRICANS brought CIVILIZATION to EUROPE

SUNDAY ADELAJA

HOW TO BECOME A developed NATION through **The DIGNITY of LABOR**

SUNDAY ADELAJA

BEST SELLING BOOKS BY DR. SUNDAY ADELAJA
AVAILABLE ON AMAZON.COM AND OKADABOOKS.COM

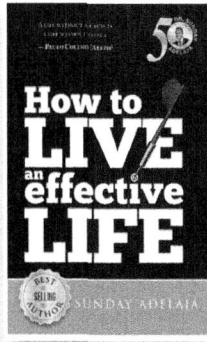

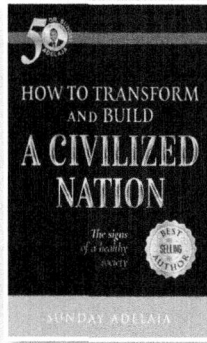

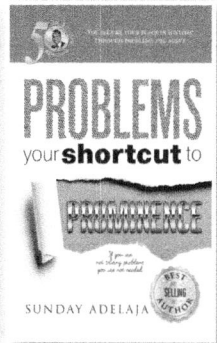

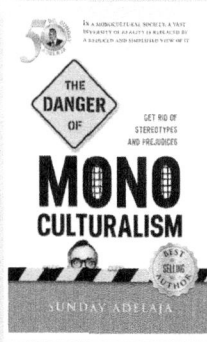

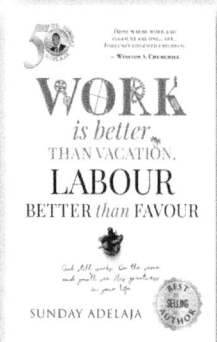

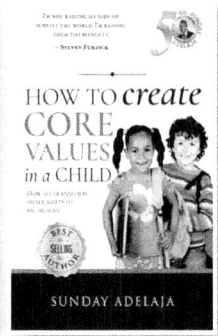

GOLDEN JUBILEE SERIES BOOKS BY DR. SUNDAY ADELAJA

1. Who Am I
2. Only God Can Save Nigeria
3. The Mountain Of Ignorance
4. Stop Working For Uncle Sam
5. Poverty Mindset Vs Abundance Mindset
6. Raising The Next Generation Of Steve Jobs And Bill Gates
7. How To Build A Secured Financial Future
8. How To Become Great Through Time Conversion
9. Create Your Own Net Worth
10. Why You Must Urgently Become A Workaholic
11. How To Regain Your Lost Years
12. Pastor, Face Your Calling
13. Discipline For Transforming Lives And Nations
14. Excellence Your Key To Elevation
15. No One Is Better Than You
16. Problems Your Shortcut To Prominence
17. Let Heroes Arise!
18. How To Live An Effective Life
19. How To Win In Life
20. The Creative And Innovative Power Of A Genius
21. The Veritable Source Of Energy
22. The Nigerian Economy. The Way Forward
23. How To Get What You Need In Life
24. 7 Tips To Self-Fulfillment
25. Life Is An Opportunity
26. The Essence And Value Of Life
27. A Visionless Life Is A Meaningless Life
28. Where There Is Problem There Is Money
29. Work Is Better Than Vacation, Labour Better Than Favour
30. How To Overcome The Fear Of Death
31. Discovering The Purpose And Calling Of Nations
32. How To Become A Developed Nation Throught The Dignity Of Labor
33. Your Greatnes Is Proportional
34. Why Losing Your Job Is The Best Thing That Could Happen To You
35. What Do You Do With Your Time
36. Life Is Predictable
37. How To Be In The Here And Now
38. I Am A Person. Am I A Personality?
39. Discover The Source Of Your Latent Energy
40. How To Form Value Systems In A Child
41. Why I Am Unlucky
42. Hello! I Am Searching For Problems
43. Holistic Personality
44. How To transform And Build a Civilized Nation
45. Could You Be The Abraham Of Your Nation
46. The teambuilding skills of Jesus
47. How to keep your focus
48. The sin of irresp5onsibility
49. How Africans Brought Civilization To Europe
50. The Danger Of Monoculturalism

FOR DISTRIBUTION OR TO ORDER BULK COPIES OF THIS BOOKS, PLEASE CONTACT US:

USA | CORNERSTONE PUBLISHING
E-mail: info@thecornerstonepublishers.com, +1 (516) 547-4999
www.thecornerstonepublishers.com

AFRICA | SUNDAY ADELAJA MEDIA LTD
E-mail: btawolana@hotmail.com
+2348187518530, +2348097721451, +2348034093699

AFRICA | CHIOMA NWIGWE (NIGERIA)
E-mail: dsabooksplanet@gmail.com • +2347065228537, +2348122219291

LONDON, UK | ADEKUNLE BANJOKO
E-mail: banjokoadekunle@gmail.com • +447411937793

KIEV, UKRAINE |
E-mail: pa@godembassy.org, Mobile: +380674401958

Printed in Great Britain
by Amazon

45697047R00111